IN THE MARGIN
OF HISTORY

PLATE I

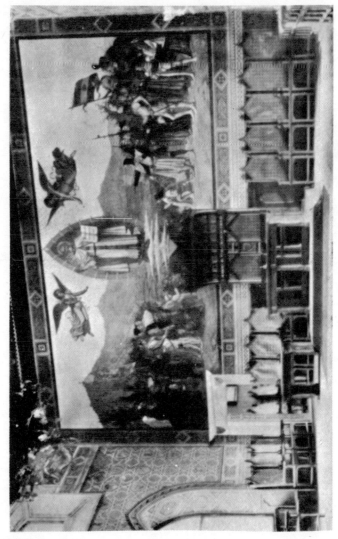

The Hall of the Great Council in the Palace of San Marino with the double throne of the Captains Regent.

IN THE MARGIN
OF HISTORY

By

SIR HARRY LUKE

Essay Index Reprint Series

BOOKS FOR LIBRARIES PRESS, INC.
FREEPORT, NEW YORK

First published 1933
Reprinted 1967

LIBRARY OF CONGRESS CATALOG CARD NUMBER:
67-26755

PRINTED IN THE UNITED STATES OF AMERICA

TO
MY SISTER
LILY BOYS

CONTENTS

ILLUSTRATIONS

ILLUSTRATIONS

MAPS AND PLANS

ACKNOWLEDGMENT

MOST of the chapters of this book have already appeared in print ; and I have to thank the Editors of *The Times*, the *Fortnightly Review*, the *Nineteenth Century and After*, the *Review of Reviews*, the *Near East and India* and the *Egyptian Gazette* for permission to reproduce them here.

For certain of the photographs not of my own taking I am indebted to Mr. H. P. Scicluna, Librarian of the Malta Public Library, Mr. A. S. Kirkbride, O.B.E., M.C., Assistant British Resident in Transjordan, and (for those of Poljica) Captain I. Gattin of Split ; while I have to thank the Gresham Committee and Mrs. Chevallier Tayler for allowing me to include the photograph of the late Mr. Chevallier Tayler's painting in the Royal Exchange of the banquet given in the Vintners' Hall to King Peter I of Cyprus and four fellow-kings.

I am grateful to Mr. H. Pirie-Gordon, D.S.C., Mr. R. T. Smallbones, M.B.E., H.B.M. Consul-General at Frankfort, Mr. N. Perić, British Vice-Consul at Split, and Professor George Andrassy of Zagreb University for information on various points ;

ACKNOWLEDGMENT

and I should like to thank Mr. C. E. Shepherd for the care which he has bestowed on the preparation of the maps.

H. C. L.

Casa dei Leoni,
Malta.

IN THE MARGIN
OF HISTORY

IN THE MARGIN OF HISTORY

FROM mediæval times, when adventurous Frankish knights carved out for themselves kingdoms and principalities in provinces wrested from the Saracen or in islands snatched from the weakening hands of the Byzantines, there have been in the West men tempted into distant and generally fantastic adventure by the lure of a crown. There was, for example, the Norman Baron de Béthencourt, who made himself King of the Canary Islands at the beginning of the fifteenth century; there was, in the sixteenth century, the strange episode of Joseph Nasi, the Jewish Duke of Naxos. Nearer to our own time was the Westphalian Baron Theodore von Neuhoff, King of Corsica, who, after exercising for a few months effective sovereignty over a considerable part of that island, spent his declining years in a London debtors' prison and found a pauper's grave at S. Anne's, Soho. Again, the struggle between England and France for supremacy in India at the close of the eighteenth century gave openings to sundry soldiers of fortune, who have been defined as soldiers who have none. The Tipperary sailor George Thomas and several Frenchmen, among whom de Boigne (husband of the authoress of the celebrated Memoirs) and one Pierre Cuiller were the most successful, seized the opportunities thus created to exalt themselves into positions more powerful, at times, than those of the native rulers whom they served. Cuiller, while nominally in the employ of the Mogul Emperor Shah Alam, struck coins in his own name; George Thomas not only struck coins but set up what was virtually an independent state in the Punjab, north-west of Delhi.

Nor did the advent of our own more prosaic era mean the end of these picturesque ambitions, even if it afforded fewer opportunities for their gratification. The nineteenth century has only witnessed one successful example of kingdom-building of this sort, that of Sarawak, but it has seen not a few attempts that have failed. It is of these attempts that I propose here to treat, in the belief that, if they have contributed nothing to history, they show that at least the world has not entirely lost its sense of humour.

Astride the Chile–Argentine frontier to the north of Patagonia lies the country of the Araucanian Indians. Never conquered by the Incas or by their successors, the Spaniards, nor as yet effectively administered by either Argentine or Chile, the Araucanians were still living under tribal conditions, and were only just beginning to be aware of the gradual encroachment by the two republics between whom they were theoretically divided on what they considered to be their independent preserves, when, in 1860, there appeared among them a Frenchman named Antony Orllie de Tounens. This de Tounens, born in 1825, was a lawyer of Périgueux of humble origin, and was generally wont to beguile the leisure of a provincial attorney's office by reading books on geography. Thus stimulated, he had conceived the project of proceeding to this no-man's-land and of organizing there some sort of colony or state which he would rule, while at the same time furthering the cultural and political interests of his native France. Selling his practice and embarking at Southampton in a British vessel, he landed in Coquimbo in August, 1858, remained there for a year learning Spanish, and then entered Araucanian territory accompanied by two compatriots, Desfontaine and La Chaise, his "Ministers" respectively of Justice and the Interior. Having established relations with some of the ruling Araucanian caciques, and having, as he declared, satisfied himself that the Araucanians preferred a monarchy to a republic (the republican régime being unpopular in their eyes as suggesting Chile and the Argentine), he issued the following Proclamation:—

"We, Prince Orllie Antony de Tounens, taking into consideration that Araucania is not subject to any other State, that it is divided into tribes, and that the interests of individuals as well as the general interest require a central Government,

"Decree as follows:—

"Article I.—A Constitutional and Hereditary

19

Monarchy is founded in Araucania. Prince Orllie
Antony de Tounens is named King.

"Article II.—Should the King not have issue,
his successors will be taken from other branches of
his family in accordance with the order of succession to be established later by Royal Decree.

"Article III.—Pending the establishment of the
principal organs of the State, Royal Decrees will
have the force of law.

"Article IV.—Our Minister, Secretary of State,
is charged with these presents.

"Done in Araucania, the 17th November, 1860.

"ORLLIE ANTONY THE FIRST."

On the same day he promulgated a lengthy Constitution,
which included provision for a Legislature elected by
universal suffrage, and he formally apprised the President of Chile of his accession to "the Throne which We
have just set up in Araucania." Three days later he
declared the annexation of Patagonia to "Our Kingdom
of Araucania." Having thus laid the foundations of
his state, Orllie now went to Valparaiso, where he spent
nine months in correspondence with friends in France,
endeavouring to secure recognition of his kingdom by
the French Government and financial support from the
French public for the realization of his schemes.
Neither was forthcoming, and the French Press refused
to take him seriously; none the less, he was determined
to persevere and in December, 1861, returned to
Araucania, raised his blue, white and green tricolour,

and was well received by gatherings of the tribes. He took the occasion to repair an omission of the previous year by instituting an hereditary peerage.

But now the Chilean Government decided to take notice of His Araucanian Majesty; an armed party was sent against him and, advised by a disloyal body-servant as to his itinerary, captured him without difficulty. For the ensuing eight months, five of which were spent on a bed of sickness, he was kept in prison, while various Chilean courts were seised of his case; finally, after many changes of venue and other delays, the Court of Santiago declared him to be insane and ordered him to be detained in an asylum—a sentence which enabled the French Consul to repatriate the unhappy King to France. His was, alas! no triumphal return; but his reply to the laughter with which the Paris Press greeted him was not without dignity or common sense: "I have been described," he wrote, "as an out-of-work king, and it has been stated that I could not return to my dominions except through the intervention of the French Government. I begin by declaring that I love my country too much to think of adding to its embarrassments, and I ask of it no other favour than to accept at my hands a colony endowed with a uniformly temperate climate, where epidemics and fevers are unheard of, a colony rich in pasturage, in forests and in mines. Where else can be found a country offering such space and opportunities for emigration? Would an out-of-work king hold such language, which has nothing of exaggeration, as I propose to show now by conclusive arguments and to-morrow by deeds? What matters the imprisonment I have undergone? If I did not fear to be misunderstood as to the import of my words, or that the greatness of the names might compromise the justice of the comparison, I would ask, in conclusion: 'Were Louis XI after Péronne, and Francis I after Pavia, any the less Kings of France than before?' The act of violence committed against me by Chile cannot affect my rights; it has only been able to suspend their exercise. . . . What I am asking for —not to increase my power but to assist the task of civilization which I have undertaken—is the emigration of honest people.

"I appeal to the disinherited of old Europe, to those whose brains or arms are unemployed, owing to the lack of a place in the sun. To the first I offer posts which will not be sinecures; to the others land which will become their property, together with sufficient capital to cover the expenses of their settlement. It is the case of a crusade worthy of the nineteenth century, of a crusade of ideas and work against ignorance. . . ."

Still determined not to abandon his projects, Orllie tried by means of appeals for men and money to reconquer his kingdom. Money was scarce, but at last he found a lawyer named Planchu who was ready to share his fortunes. The first social intercourse of the King and his new Minister did not, it is true, augur any too well for the smoothness of their future relations.

"Some days after I had made Planchu's acquaintance," writes Orllie, "he invited me to dinner. The meal passed off without incident; I was his guest. None the less, I remarked that, when dispensing the various dishes, he retained the best pieces for himself, especially in the case of a roast fowl, of which he served me with the leg while himself keeping the wing. 'Here is a Minister,' I said to myself, 'who is far from treating me as a King.'"

However, the pair set out for Buenos Aires in 1869, eluded both Argentine and Chilean authorities and, after crossing the Cordilleras and enduring great hardships, entered Araucania. Despite an absence of over seven years, Orllie was well received by the Indians, and, had he but disposed of a moderate supply of arms and money, it is probable that he might have maintained himself for some time among them and have proved a real menace to the Chilean Government. Even as it was, he held on until the middle of 1871, when increasing Chilean pressure and the exhaustion of his resources, together with differences with Planchu, necessitated another temporary withdrawal. But at Marseilles, whither he retired for the time being, he published a journal in the interests of his cause, bestowed on those prepared to defray the necessary fees the Order of the Crown of Steel, which he had founded during his second "reign," and published, under the title "Love-letter to marriageable young ladies," an invitation to share his throne. The qualifications to be possessed by the young woman were: (1) honesty and membership of a respectable family; (2) excellent health, good character, intelligence, a good education and good looks; (3) the sharing of his royal tastes.

In 1874 this indefatigable man made a third attempt to establish himself in his "domains." But this time he was arrested at sea by an Argentine man-of-war after having left Buenos Aires for some spot along the coast, was taken back to Buenos Aires and lodged in prison, and was then deported to France. The unhappy king now at last lost heart and died, broken in health and spirits, four years later.

Orllie de Tounens was not a wholly ludicrous personage. Some of his schemes were, no doubt, fantastic; but his idea of founding a state in what was to a certain extent a no-man's-land, in a territory at all events not effectively occupied by any acknowledged Power, was not necessarily hopeless. Had his persistence, his energy and his force of character been matched by equally good fortune, he might have become in the end something more than an object of pity or derision.

Another piece of South American territory of indeterminate political status gave rise to similar incidents about the same period. For almost two centuries prior to 1900 the region of Counani to the south-west of French Guiana was in dispute between France and Portugal, and subsequently with Brazil, to whom it was in that year entirely attributed under the award of an arbitrator. But in the middle of the nineteenth century

24

it was another no-man's-land, maintaining a chaotic existence as a buffer between the two contesting parties. It possessed a very small white population, chiefly consisting of gold miners, who lived in rough wooden shanties and paid ten grammes of gold for a tin of sardines. In 1874 a genial Frenchman named Prosper Chaton discovered on a map that this territory appeared to belong to no one, and issued a declaration to the effect that he was the owner of it—a declaration which evoked no protest from Counani in view of the fact that it never became known there. One evening Monsieur Chaton, who was a gambler, lost his dominions at cards, and Monsieur Paul Cartier, who was a better piquet player than Monsieur Chaton, thus became the second President of the Free State of Counani.

On the subject of Monsieur Cartier's reign history is unfortunately silent, and Counani disappears from the limelight until the end of the eighteen-eighties, when some of its white inhabitants, having failed to persuade the Governor of French Guiana to declare a French Protectorate over the disputed territory, decided to set up an independent Government and invited a French journalist named Jules Gros to accept the presidency. Monsieur Gros, "publicist, Officer of the Academy, Member of the Geographical Societies of Paris, Rouen and Lisbon, Municipal Councillor of Vanves, etc.," accepted the offer, and announced to the world, through the columns of the *Journal Officiel de Counani*, that the seat of the Government of the Republic had been set up in Paris at 18, Rue du Louvre. The new President appointed a Ministry and founded, as was only to be expected, an Order of Chivalry denominated the Star of Counani; while the Emperor of Brazil, Dom Pedro II, extended his habitual good-nature so far as to receive his rival in the course of one of his visits to Paris.

It was not long before internal Cabinet dissensions manifested themselves at 18, Rue du Louvre. The Secretary of State, who bore the ominous name of Guignes, having been divested of his functions for insisting that Ministers should appear publicly in Paris in the full dress uniform which he had devised for them, retaliated by endeavouring to depose the President. Thereupon the President, who had not hitherto set foot in his dominions, bethought himself seriously of transferring his activities to Counani, despite the circumstance that the French and Brazilian Governments had issued an official statement describing the establishment of "the so-called Republic of Counani" as unauthorized. He formed a syndicate in England, to which he granted the right to exploit the resources of the Republic, and in August, 1888, landed in Georgetown, British Guiana. Here he embarked in a vessel which, he believed, was taking him to his capital; but, alas! her perfidious master, who suspected that a French man-of-war was contemplating pursuit of the President, diverted her course by proceeding, without any farther calls, directly to London.

The spiriting away of Monsieur Gros, far from

bringing the series of Presidents of Counani to an abrupt end, prepared the field for a fresh crop of these potentates. The arbitral award of the territory to Brazil, unwelcome in France, was equally unwelcome in Counani, whose inhabitants were anything but pleased at the advent of courts of law and other adjuncts of a regular administration. A French ex-private of marines named Adolphe Brezet, who had served in French Guiana, proclaimed himself, in 1901, President of the Independent State of Counani, assumed the name of Uayana Assu, which presumably has a true Counanian ring, and issued a Constitution of thirty-seven articles establishing various constitutional bodies. Roman Catholicism was declared to be the religion of the State, and arms, motto and flag were not forgotten. Neither were there forgotten the means of rewarding the benefactors and servants of the republic, as witness the rapid creation of the Orders of the Holy Ghost, of the Cross of Palestine, of Our Lady of Good Help, the Military Iron Cross, the Order of Commercial Merit, and the Agricultural Order of S. Fiacre. It was a syndicate for the commercial development of the republic that caused Monsieur Brezet to transfer his activities from Paris to London on the day that the French courts were proceeding to an investigation of the syndicate's financial operations. It was in London that the President may be said to have exercised to their fullest extent his sovereign powers. He set up a consulate and appointed a consul, whose first task it was to grant to his President a decree of divorce from his wife and to unite him *en secondes noces* with a charming young Frenchwoman. Who shall say that Monsieur Brezet's presidential swan-song was not an effective one?

Before leaving South America let us bestow a glance on the Principality of Trinidad and on its sovereign, James I by the Grace of God Prince thereof. His late Highness, born in San Francisco in 1854 plain James Aloysius Harden-Hickey, was the son of an Irishman who had made money in the Californian gold rush. When he was still a young man his parents established themselves in Paris, and young Harden-Hickey entered the French Military College of Saint Cyr. A kick from a horse, which severely lamed him, nipping his military career in the bud, Harden-Hickey launched forth into social activities which entailed his financial ruin, and into political and journalistic activities which entailed his banishment from France. He now set out for the Spanish Main in search of farther adventure, married an heiress, and in due course happened upon the small island of Trinidad (not to be confused with the large West Indian island of the same name), which lies 680 miles east of the coast of Espirito Santo, Brazil, and was subsequently, in 1895, to be claimed by both the British and the Brazilian Governments before being finally adjudicated to the latter. This Trinidad, four miles long by two miles in breadth, was only inhabited, it is true, by wild pigs and a few goats, but Harden-

Hickey was not to be prevented by considerations such as these from doing his duty by the island of his choice. In September, 1893, he announced to the Great Powers his elevation to its throne under the title of James the First. No republics or parliaments for this ex-cadet of Saint Cyr! A military dictatorship was the chosen form of government; but, lest intending settlers should be deterred thereby, corresponding inducements were held out to the enterprising by the Chancery of the Principality, established at 217, West 36th Street, New York City. Rich deposits of guano were only awaiting removal; the treasure of the Cathedral of Lima, abstracted from Peruvian territory in the course of an insurrection and understood to have been hidden by pirates in Trinidad in 1825, could not fail to be found by earnest seekers; while for those who preferred to assist in the development of the principality from their own homes there remained the handsome yellow and red ribbon of the Order of the Cross of Trinidad, whose three classes were bestowed for the trifling sums of £40, £80 and £120 respectively.

"Put not your trust in princes" may have been the reaction of those to whom his Highness James I addressed his appeal. The Principality of Trinidad fell flat, and poor Harden-Hickey committed suicide in Texas in 1898.

Among the aborigines whom the Annamese and other dominant races of Indo-China have gradually driven from the coast into the interior and generically call

Mois, a word meaning "savages," is the tribe of the Sedangs, a people to whom a picturesque French adventurer gave a temporary notoriety in the 'seventies and 'eighties of the last century. Charles Louis Mary David de Mayrena was born at Toulon in 1841, served as quite a young man in a regiment of Spahis in Cochin-China, left the French Army in 1868, rejoined for the Franco-Prussian War, and then returned to Indo-China, where for some years he lived more or less obscurely, exploring, searching for gold and rubber, and occasionally employed on demi-official missions by the French administration. In the course of one of these missions, in which it was his task to watch and so far as possible to counteract the activities of certain Germans whose presence in the interior was exercising the French Government, Mayrena found himself in the country of the Sedangs, who had not yet come under the control of the French. These Sedangs seem to have had some sort of loose confederation of chiefs, whose goodwill Mayrena managed to secure; and his next step was to emit the following admirably succinct Proclamation:—

"Art. 1.—The Republic of the Sedangs is erected into a Monarchy.

"Art. 2.—Charles Mary de Mayrena is proclaimed King of this nation under the name of Mary I."

It should be made clear that Mayrena's assumption of the royal dignity was not in conflict with the interests of the French, whose delimited frontiers were then well outside what he was pleased to consider to be his dominions. Indeed, he received, so late as 1888, an official letter from the Governor-General of Indo-China congratulating him upon the success of his contribution towards the opening up of the interior, while he had also been helped from time to time by the Jesuit Fathers of some of the inland missions. But, as in the case of many another monarch, finance proved his undoing. The paper money which he issued seemed somehow to be unable to maintain its face value, his Order of S. Margaret was not very much in demand, and, finally, there was a difficulty about the signatures to certain bills of exchange which had been negotiated by His Majesty.

Mayrena thought it prudent to withdraw for the time being from the Far East. *Via* Paris, therefore, where he ordered a supply of postage stamps, he proceeded to Brussels, where he spent the ensuing few months in raising money on the mineral worth of his kingdom and in fitting out an expedition to his Sedangs. An enthusiastic supporter advanced him 200,000 francs, and with this capital he chartered a vessel and put to sea. But his ship was so full of arms that she was stopped at Singapore by the British authorities, who duly apprised the French of the circumstances of Mayrena's return. This time the French would have nothing to do with him, and forbade him to land in Indo-China. The disconsolate king then wandered about among some of the small East Indian islands, doing such business as he could with petty Malay sultans, and died soon afterwards, either from snakebite or at the hands of a native.

Mayrena had rightly seen where his opportunity lay, and he lacked neither courage nor enterprise. Had he not been as unprincipled and dishonest as he was undoubtedly intelligent, he might well have carved out for himself a second Sarawak in the vacuum that had not yet been filled by the advance of the French to the Siamese borders.

The potentates whose careers we have been considering have all, at some time or another, been hard put to it to raise the funds required for the maintenance of their dominions and dignities. Some of them, indeed, have even had to resort to methods which brought them into conflict with the police. We now come to two personages whose resources made it easy for them to gratify their regal proclivities.

In the early years of the twentieth century Europe was amused by the antics of the son of a wealthy sugar manufacturer named Lebaudy, whose eccentricities, committed under the style and title of James the First, Emperor of the Sahara, added for a while to the gaiety of nations. This humorist, taking note of the circumstance that the western part of the Sahara desert was but sparsely populated and even less noticeably administered by the Powers among which it was at all events nominally divided (the "Empire" lay mostly within the

Spanish territory of Rio de Oro), considered it a suitable venue for the empire which he proposed to establish. Setting sail in his yacht *Frasquita*, which was well found with crew, stores, arms, a Minister of State and even an empress, Lebaudy proceeded on the 23rd May, 1903, towards the coast of Rio de Oro. On the morning of the second day at sea he issued an order to his crew henceforth to address him as Captain, a little later in the day as General, and before the day was out as Majesty, or as Sire. The crew, being under-worked and well paid, raised no objection to complying with what they regarded as the harmless whims of their owner; and it was as His Imperial Majesty that he landed in the neighbourhood of Cape Juby and proceeded to demarcate his future capital of Troja.

For the moment the Imperial family and staff were accommodated in tents, but a portable palace was already on order from England, as well as a portable stable. The stable was to be no ordinary one, for the Emperor possessed no ordinary imagination. His study of Saharan conditions had led him to the regrettable conclusion that that noble animal, the horse—albeit admirable in every respect in temperate climes and on suitable soil—was incapable of coping adequately with the shifting sands of the desert; while, on the other hand, that patient and enduring beast, the camel, lacked the quality—so essential in the service of Empire-builders—of speed. If, however, the two strains could be crossed so as to produce a hybrid that would combine the speed of one parent with the endurance over sand of the other, the problem of Saharan transport was solved; and it was to this end, namely that of producing a new animal to be called *"cha-val,"* that the Imperial stables were designed. Moreover, the Emperor, on his return to Europe, caused the following notice to be inserted in the European Press:—

> "His Majesty, anxious to encourage sport, offers a prize of 500,000 francs in connexion with the forthcoming racing season at Troja."

It is to be regretted that the political development of the Saharan Empire was such as to nip in the bud these interesting experiments.

Into the difficulties and litigation in which the Emperor subsequently found himself involved with his staff—into the details of the unilateral negotiations upon which he embarked with the Government of Morocco—into his attempts to induce the Hague Tribunal to take cognizance of his claims, it is needless here to enter. Pursuing his imperial ambitions with great fixity of purpose but in diverse ways, he moved from capital to capital and towards the latter part of 1903 was keeping his Court in London. A relative of mine, lunching at the Savoy one day in December of that year, brought me back the following document, copies of which had been distributed by the Imperial aides-de-camp throughout the hotel, then patronized by the Emperor:—

"EMPIRE DU SAHARA.
AVIS AU PUBLIC.

Il est, par la présente, porté à la connaissance du public, qu'à partir du Ier Janvier, 1904, le nom de JACQUES LEBAUDY ne devra plus être employé et devra être remplacé par celui de

JACQUES Ier.

En effet Sa Majesté JACQUES Ier a renoncé complètement à Son nom de famille pour se conformer aux lois de l'Empire du Sahara réglant l'Etat-Civil.

Toute lettre adressée à Sa Majesté doit l'être comme suit:

A SA MAJESTÉ JACQUES Ier,
EMPEREUR DU SAHARA.

Quand Sa Majesté est dans Ses Etats, indiquer comme résidence:

AU PALAIS IMPERIAL DE TROJA.

Quand Elle est en dehors de Ses Etats, indiquer simplement la ville où Sa Majesté a établi Sa résidence.

Quant au refus intentionnel de donner à Sa Majesté Ses titres il sera interprété comme un acte discourtois et entrainera la rupture des relations de Sa Majesté avec son auteur.

Les nombreux correspondents de Sa Majesté sont priés de vouloir bien se conformer aux indications ci-dessus."

One of the last official acts of His Imperial Majesty, before inevitable bankruptcy overtook him, was to despatch, through his "Minister for Foreign Affairs," a Moor who called himself Tewfik Pasha, a formal protest to Monsieur Rouvier, the French Prime Minister, against the omission to invite the Government of the Sahara to send a plenipotentiary to the Algeciras Conference.

The name of Cyprus in the south-eastern corner of the Mediterranean is still redolent of the romance with which it was invested during the three hundred years when the kings and queens of the House of Lusignan maintained in that lovely island what was in effect a continuation of Crusading rule after the Crusaders had been finally expelled from the Holy Land itself. What student of mediæval history has not delighted in the romantic story of King Peter I of Cyprus, the greatest knight-errant the world has seen—has not read with emotion the chronicles of the struggle for the Cypriote crown between Queen Carlotta and her bastard brother James —has not deplored the hard fate of the beautiful Katharine Cornaro, the island's last independent sovereign? It was many centuries ago that this most picturesque of dynasties disappeared from history; but, if the reader will look at the *Almanach de Gotha* for 1889 (he will find the reference in no other year), he will see that, phœnix-like, it had seemed to rise from its ashes. For he will observe there, described as the "head of the Catholic branch" of that House, the name

36

of one Prince Guy de Lusignan, with that of his wife, the Princess Marie, *née* Countess de Godefroy le Goupil. In effect this lady, as charitable as she was wealthy and as wealthy as she was romantic, decided to resurrect the mediæval Orders of Chivalry of the dynasty from which her husband claimed descent—the Order of the Sword, the Order of Melusine (Melusine was a beauteous mermaid and the legendary ancestress of the House of Lusignan), and I know not what else besides—and proceeded to confer them, in their several classes, upon those persons who were prepared to subscribe to her charities. The Princess Marie, it must be admitted, did things well, and her decorations were made by the best goldsmiths in the Palais Royal. Their heraldry is accurate, their gold, silver and enamel work is beyond praise; and, even if they were not recognized at Courts, or in salons other than those of the Princess Marie, they must at all events have embellished very considerably the appearance of their wearers.

It might be thought that in this disillusioned postwar world of ours, face to face as it is with stern realities, there would be no room for the amiable triflers with whom this chapter has, in part at all events, been concerned. That such is not the case is proved by a Proclamation, a copy of which lies before me as I write, headed and terminated by a superb heraldic achievement. As this document seems to shed a distinct gleam of joy upon our murky age, I append a

37

translation, from the French original, of its essential parts. It is headed: "Anniversary of the Foundation of the Domanial Kingdom of Transcaucasia-Vitanvali: Proclamation of the King to the Transcaucasians, Georgians, Caucasians and members of the former Committee of Independence and of the Foundation of the Kingdom." I may perhaps be allowed to mention that, notwithstanding two fairly prolonged periods of residence in Transcaucasia, I had never heard of the Kingdom of Vitanvali before the Proclamation came to my notice; but I find that this circumstance in no wise robs the document of its charm. After recalling (it is dated Bordighera, the 5th December, 1921) that it is a year since King Louis I was elected and proclaimed hereditary King of Transcaucasia-Vitanvali and the independence of the kingdom was notified to all the Powers, including the League of Nations, it proceeds:—

"Notwithstanding the grave events which have taken place in Russia since this date, and the arbitrary arrest of your King in violation of the Rights of Peoples by a Foreign Power instigated thereto by a perverse and factious Minister jealous of your independence and worthy disciple of Rasputin, you have remained faithful to Our cause and to Our person.

"On the morrow of the trial which restored to Us Our personal liberty but obliged Us, on the 25th October, 1921, by Decree countersigned by Our Secretary of State, Minister of Foreign Affairs of the Kingdom, to repudiate the Grand Duchess of Maikop, Clementine Faroppa, whom we had thought worthy to be raised to this title as Royal fiancée but now recognize as undeserving of Our confidence and of reigning at Our side, We have been advised by a European Power that, in order to guarantee Our independence and to assure Our legitimate and legal sovereignty over Transcaucasia-Vitanvali, it is necessary that we should be protected without delay by a powerful State capable of enforcing respect towards Us. Having therefore submitted proposals for the basis of a Protectorate to the British Government, under whose protection we had from the very beginning spontaneously placed Our Royal and Domanial Government, We have now informed His Excellency Mr. Lloyd George, the Prime Minister, and His Excellency the Marquess Curzon of Kedleston, Minister of Foreign Affairs, that Our Secretary of State, Minister of Foreign Affairs of the Kingdom, Count Suteroff, has been charged with a diplomatic mission abroad in order to negotiate a Protectorate with one of the Great Powers, on the lines of that submitted to the British Ministers, in the event of Great Britain not giving a favourable answer to Our proposals.

"In order to give to Our Secretary of State all possible authority and to reward him for his mission so happily undertaken, we confer on Count Arnold Suter de Suteroff, Minister of State and of Foreign Affairs, the titles of Marquis of Sabeva and Grand Cross of the White Eagle.

39

"Our Ministers Duke Alexis Dokoudowsky, the Marquis de Carmo, Count Costech de Yavorsky, Count Nicholas Grigorieff, are appointed Peers of the Kingdom and Members of the Privy Council of the Crown.

"I thank Prince Molchanoff Kazyne-Bek, Councillor of State, who had the goodness, out of friendship to Us, to come to the aid of Our ex-fiancée during Our captivity on her behalf, having been deceived by her wily hypocrisy and her lack of heart. Let all Russians be reassured: she is nothing more and will never again be anything more to Us."

Such are the principal contents of this remarkable Proclamation, with its tale of political and domestic contrarieties. Some people, we know, struck oil in Maikop. Evidently Louis I, King of Transcaucasia-Vitanvali, was not among them.

FREAKS OF
FREEDOM

II

FREAKS OF FREEDOM

I

It is only within comparatively recent times that the little countries which have preserved their independence from an earlier age into our own day have begun to assume the appearance of political curiosities, of territorial midgets. In the ancient Hellenic world the independent city state was the normal framework of political life, the vast agglomerations of the empires of Persia and Rome the exception. In mediæval Italy the number of city republics and petty principalities far exceeded that of the larger entities such as the kingdom of Naples. The Hanse towns, now reduced to Lübeck, Hamburg and Bremen but once much more numerous, are examples of the sovereign city states in Northern Europe. The Holy Roman Empire—which, be it remembered, survived until 1806—embraced no fewer than 173 secular and ecclesiastical monarchies, many of them little more extensive than a large country estate, and fifty-one free cities. The component parts of that modern creation, the German Empire, were twenty-five sovereign and coin-issuing kingdoms, Grand

Duchies, Duchies, Principalities and cities, including fourteen with areas under one thousand square miles, of which ten were under five hundred. And so far is the principle of small sovereign entities from being considered incompatible with the ideas of to-day that the Treaty of Versailles actually created two new specimens: the territory of Memel, which was detached from Germany by the treaty and placed under the control of the Conference of Ambassadors until, in 1923, it was transferred to Lithuania, and the Free City of Danzig, which seems likely to endure.

It is really only where the miniature states are rendered conspicuous by geographical isolation, either by being set in the territory of a larger country, as are Monaco and San Marino, or by being wedged between two greater neighbours, as are Liechtenstein and Andorra, that their smallness is brought into high relief and has caused some of the writers who have concerned themselves with their affairs to apply to them the description I have borrowed for the title of this chapter, that of "Freaks of Freedom." Whether in point of fact they are or are not freer than their larger neighbours is a matter of opinion which I do not propose to discuss. It is also a problem of metaphysics, since it must necessarily lead to the unprofitable question: What is freedom? The thing that is noteworthy is the contrast in régime which they provide. Thus, Monaco is a monarchy surrounded by a republic, San Marino a republic in the middle of a monarchy. It is only since

44

the Spanish revolution that Andorra has been bounded on both sides by sister-republics; while Liechtenstein is not only a monarchy placed between two republics but is proud to proclaim itself the only surviving monarchy in Central Europe.

The oldest of these political curiosities, in fact, the oldest secular state in Europe, is the republic of San Marino, which is situated in Central Italy, on the Adriatic slope of the Apennines, and, surrounded on all sides by Italian territory, has been described not inaptly as "a mole on the cheek of a fair lady." The republic is thirty-two square miles in extent and has a frontier line of twenty-four miles, with a population of some 13,000. Its little capital, also named San Marino, overlooks the great highway of nations which was once the Via Emilia from the summit of Monte Titano, that

> "Alto Titano, ove lo stanco piede
> Raccolse libertade, e s'ebbe nome
> Dal suo Divin Marin."

Ten miles to the north-east, on the coast, appears the ancient city of Rimini, to which the eye is carried by the stony river-bed of the Marecchia; to the south lies the territory of the former Duchy of Urbino, which was wont to afford its powerful and benevolent protection to its little neighbour. The republic of Monte Titano, surmounted by the three crags, each crowned by its feathered tower, which are its heraldic achievement, was once one of the least of those many small yet vigorous independent states which,

45

"Like rocks which fire lifts out of the flat deep,
    Arose in sacred Italy,
    Frowning o'er the tempestuous sea
    Of kings, and priests, and slaves, in tower-crowned majesty."

To-day it is their sole survivor, and its vitality cannot
be explained more succinctly than in the words of the

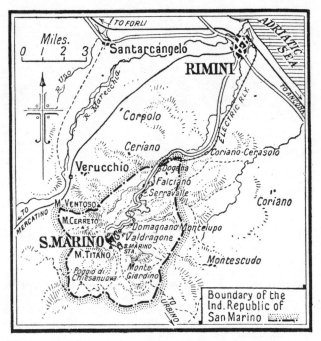

Frenchman who wrote: "*La République de St. Marin
n'est ni redoutée, ni redoutable, telle est la cause de sa
longue prosperité.*" Indeed, it is not only because the
abrupt and rugged slopes of Monte Titano afford magnificent natural protection to the little state that it is

alive to-day, but because the republic has been too poor, too simple, too rustic to attract the invader. It is one of the minor ironies of history that while the splendid signories of Venice, of Florence, of Genoa, of Siena and countless others, each with their traditions, their robust individualities, their schools of painting and architecture, should have merged their separate political entity into a greater whole, the only contemporary to retain it should be an obscure group of nine humble country parishes.[1]

The origin of the republic is ascribed to a Christian Dalmatian stonemason named Marinus who, leaving his native island of Arbe early in the fourth century to help in the rebuilding of Rimini which had been ordered by Diocletian, and involved in the Emperor's persecution of the Christians, took refuge on Monte Titano, where he could hew his stone and practise his religion unmolested. A community soon grew up around the hermitage of Marinus, who had now become a deacon and was afterwards to become a saint, and grew by degrees into one of those small, free communes characteristic of mediæval Italy. Although the independence of the little republic was not formally codified for some time, its motto, *"Libertas,"* was evidently already its watchword, for among the archives of the republic is a document relating to an inquiry ordered into the affairs of Monte Titano in the

---

[1] Seven of the parishes are ecclesiastically within the diocese of Montefeltro (Pennabilli), two in that of Rimini.

thirteenth century by Pope Boniface VIII. The investigator asked of the citizens what they meant by their "liberty." He was answered thus: "It means that we belong to ourselves, that we owe no homage to anyone amongst ourselves, but only to the Master of all things." Throughout the ensuing centuries of turbulence and wars in the rest of Italy, San Marino pursued its humble, unprovocative way in peace, consolidating its sovereign status and prudently "escaping notice." In fact, the most serious attempt on its independence was made as recently as 1739, by Cardinal Alberoni, then the Papal Legate in the Romagna. Alberoni, who had once been the virtual dictator of Spain, which he had left after the failure of his plan to unite Sardinia and Sicily to the Spanish Crown, was apparently content to seek consolation for his discomfiture in the annexation of poor little San Marino to the States of the Church. Once more he failed, causing Pope Benedict XIV, who reaffirmed the independence of the republic, to remark that Alberoni was like a glutton who, after a good dinner, would fain have some brown bread.

Another critical moment came later, when Napoleon played havoc with the political and dynastic organization of the Peninsula. But here again San Marino was unique, for alone of the Italian States it was befriended by the conqueror, who declared that it should be preserved *comme échantillon de république* and behaved towards it, in the apt expression of Theodore Bent, "like a capricious giant caressing a dwarf." He not only refrained from incorporating it in the Department of the Rubicon of his ephemeral kingdom of Italy; he actually promised it a present of four cannon for the citadel. What if he forgot to send the guns? He gave it the inestimably greater gift of sparing its life.

For a third time, before it entered into its present era of security, circumstances outside its control brought the republic into contact with events which might have endangered its existence but which, in accordance with its proverbial good fortune, did but enhance its reputation.

At the end of November, 1848, Pius IX, who had begun his reign as the idol of the Liberals and was to end it as the embodiment of reaction and the spirit of *non possumus*, having refused to fight Austria and broken with the leaders of the *Risorgimento*, fled from Rome to Gaeta in the kingdom of Naples. His departure made possible the proclamation of the Roman Republic, whose defence against the troops sent by Napoleon III in aid of the exiled Pope was entrusted to Garibaldi. Despite the efforts of the infant republic the French entered Rome on the 2nd July, 1849, while Garibaldi and his followers escaped to the north. His plan was to make for one of the Adriatic ports and there to embark his 1,500 men for friendly Venice, then also a republic under Daniele Manin; but, before he could do so, he was held up by the troops of the Austrian Archduke Ernest outside the little town of Sant' Angelo in Vado, a few miles to the west of Urbino. Two other

Austrian armies were moving on him from the west and north respectively, and Garibaldi had to make the choice between surrender and of seeking refuge in the neutral territory of San Marino. Accordingly, he sent his quartermaster to the Captains Regent to announce his arrival and to request a safe passage and victuals for his troops, receiving the reluctant reply that if he passed through San Marino he would violate his principles by endangering the existence of a republic without doing himself any good. For the Sammarinesi could see with the naked eye from Monte Titano the Austrians surrounding their country on all sides. Nevertheless, they promised to place food for the Redshirts at the boundaries of the republic. But with Garibaldi it was a case of *force majeure;* he had now no option but to enter the republic uninvited and to throw himself on the mercy of its citizens. On the morning of the 31st July, 1849, he arrived in the capital and was received by the Captains Regent and the Council.

"Captains Regent," said the General; "my troops, pursued by superior numbers of Austrians, and exhausted by the privations they have endured among the mountains and precipices, are no longer in a condition to fight; it therefore became necessary to cross your border to obtain bread and a few hours' repose. They shall lay down their arms in your republic, where the Roman war for the independence of Italy now comes to an end. I come among you as a refugee; receive me as such."

As refugees, therefore, the Garibaldians were received in San Marino, whose Government agreed to mediate with the Austrians to secure their capitulation. Meanwhile, Garibaldi posted up on the walls of the Collegiate Church the last Order of the Day of the campaign. It ran as follows:—

"Republic of San Marino.

"Order of the Day, July 31, 1849, 2 p.m.

"Soldiers,—We have reached the land of refuge, and we owe the best behaviour to our generous hosts. We, too, have earned the consideration due to persecuted misfortune.

"From this moment forward I release my companions from all obligation, and leave you free to return to private life. But remember that Italy must not continue in shame, and that it is better to die than to live as slaves of the foreigner.

"GARIBALDI."

Into the negotiations between the Government of San Marino and the Archduke Ernest there is no space here to enter. Suffice it to say that the Archduke ultimately agreed that, subject to the confirmation of the Austrian Commander-in-Chief at Bologna, the Garibaldians were to surrender their arms to the Sammarinesi, who were to hand them over to the Austrians, whereupon the disarmed men were to be allowed to return unmolested to their homes with the exception of Garibaldi and his wife, who were to depart for America. But Garibaldi could not bring himself personally to accept these terms. While the Austrians were awaiting the reply of the Captains Regent, Garibaldi, with his wife Anita, who refused to leave him although she was all but exhausted by the privations of the retreat and was to die a few weeks later, and about 180 of his most trusted followers, escaped quietly to the little seaport of Cesenatico, leaving behind him the following laconic message:—

> "Citizens of the Republic,
> "The conditions imposed on me by the Austrians are unacceptable, and therefore we cease to encumber your territory.
> "GARIBALDI."

The Austrians were exasperated to find that Garibaldi had escaped from their clutches, and the Captain Regent, whom the Sammarinesi hastily despatched to the Archduke, had much difficulty to persuade the latter to acquit the republic of connivance. "At length, however," says Theodore Bent, in his book on San Marino,

> "the Austrian general was appeased, and nothing but polite messages passed between the Austrians and the Sammarinesi; the Archduke asking leave to remove his soldiers into more comfortable quarters, and the Sammarinesi inviting him to bring them all to the Borgo, whilst the Archduke himself was to be lodged in the house of the Conte Borghese in the Città. Nothing loth to accept this hospitality, the Austrian general took this

opportunity to rest his army for a few days, and made himself most agreeable to the inhabitants, receiving deputations, and inquiring into the constitution of the republic, gracefully vouchsafing to admire everything he saw therein. Much, however, as they may personally have liked their guest, the Sammarinesi thought fit to offer up a Te Deum in their church on his departure, as a thanksgiving for their escape from so many dangers. . . . But this little episode in their history cost the republic no small sum of money; their commissariat was drained again and again, and the inhabitants not infrequently felt the pangs of hunger, having so many mouths to fill, as, of course, there was no one to repay them for their outlay; but they were contented in their humble minds to have been instrumental in saving the life of one so dear to Italian freedom as Garibaldi."

The subsequent years of San Marino's history have been happy and uneventful. In 1862 it entered into a treaty of commerce and alliance with United Italy, subsequently renewed, and in 1864 issued its first coin, a bronze *soldo*. Other bronze coins were struck on four subsequent occasions, and in 1898 the republic issued its first silver coinage with pieces of a half lira, and one, two and five lire. More silver of the same design was issued in 1906, while at the end of 1931 there began the issue of a new silver coinage, which by treaty is legal tender in Italy and in the Vatican City. San Marino has had its own postage stamps since 1877; and in

1932 was completed the electric railway of thirty-two kilometres connecting it with Rimini, of which twenty kilometres are in the territory of the republic.

I visited San Marino nearly thirty years ago, when the normal means of reaching it was in a humble one-horse *vettura*. My companion and I had provided ourselves with an official introduction to the Captains Regent from the Minister of San Marino in Paris (there was none in London) and, although this precaution was probably unnecessary, since the Sammarinesi welcome the interested stranger, it perhaps opened official doors that might otherwise have been closed. The two Captains Regent were as kind and hospitable as they could be, while the Secretary of State for Foreign Affairs, who was also Postmaster-General, conducted us personally over the attractive new Palazzo Pubblico, which is an admirable reproduction of the mediæval Italian communal palace, and into the archives of the republic. He also showed us the seventeenth-century state dress of doublet and trunk hose which the Captains Regent wear at their installation. The Constitution of the republic is as interesting a survival as is the republic itself. The repository of sovereignty is the assembly originally consisting of the heads of families and called the Arringo, which has now been standardized into the "Prince and Sovereign Council" (*Consiglio Principe e Sovrano*) of sixty members, twenty patricians, twenty townsmen and twenty countrymen. Elected by the Sovereign Council is the Council of Twelve, which is in

PLATE II

The three feathered Towers of San Marino.

The old Palazzo Pubblico of San Marino, now
demolished and replaced by the new Palazzo.

To face p. 54.

a sense like our House of Lords in that it has not only legislative but judicial functions. The State is represented by its two Captains Regent, jointly elected for a period of six months from among the Sovereign Council and only eligible for re-election after an interval of three years. One regent is chosen from among the patricians, one from either of the other classes, and on the double throne in the *Sala del Consiglio* the noble Regent sits on the right, his plebeian colleague on the left. But by a pleasing touch the position is reversed in the Collegiate Church, where, in the sight of God, all men are equal. On this throne, on the Gospel side of the altar, it is the non-noble who sits on the right.

We must not expect to find a long list of celebrities produced by this small community of peasants, but here and there a name stands out from amongst those of merely local worthies. One of the great military engineers of the sixteenth century was a certain Giambattista Belluzzi, a member of one of the most prominent families of the republic, who served Cosimo de' Medici as State Engineer of Florence and actually travelled professionally as far afield as Scotland. The birthplace of the painter and architect Bramante is variously ascribed to the territory of the republic and to that of the adjoining duchy of Urbino; and I recently lighted by accident, not in any of the fairly numerous histories of San Marino,[1] upon a Sammarinese

[1] The standard work is the *Memorie Storiche della Repubblica di San Marino* by the Cavaliere Melchiorre Delfico, first published in 1804, with several later editions.

55

Prince of the Church who played a not inconspicuous part in Vatican affairs in the first half of the nineteenth century. This was Cardinal Gamberini, a creation of Leo XII. The Conclave which elected Leo's successor, Pius VIII, was watched on behalf of Charles X of France by the great Chateaubriand, who once, incidentally, coined the happy epigram: "*Je suis monarchiste en France, et républicain à St. Marin.*" Simultaneously with the secret notes on the Conclave supplied by Chateaubriand to his royal master there reached the Quai d'Orsay certain other confidential sketches of the cardinals attending it, drawn up by a former secretary of Talleyrand named d'Hauterive. From these sketches I translate some of the lines relating to his Eminence of San Marino:

> "Cardinal Gamberini was born in the republic of San Marino, an imperceptible State which, on account of its smallness, has contrived to remain unnoticed by even the narrow politics of Italy. Cardinal Gamberini is, by reason of his learning, of the refinement of his language and manners and of his perfect courtesy, the most brilliant member of the Sacred College."

This paragon, by no means as imperceptible as his native country, became joint Papal Secretary of State under Gregory XVI.

Among the literary lights who have cast their beam on the little republic is George Sand, who wrote the preface to a book on San Marino brought out in 1865 by a certain Monsieur de Bougy. Comparing San Marino with its sister republic of Andorra she issues a warning to those who might expect to find them similar in every respect. "The history of Andorra," she says,

> "is patriarchal; that of San Marino, heroic. Andorra is a peaceful municipality solidly built; San Marino, a fortress and a sort of church. For my part, I do not hesitate to give my entire preference to San Marino if only because, at all times of danger and strife, its rock has been the asylum of the exiled and the oppressed, while the good peasants of Andorra have been hospitable only to those whose presence brought them neither trouble nor danger."

Let us see to what extent her criticism is true by turning our attention to that relic of feudalism in the Pyrenees.

The full designation of this State is "the Republic of the Valleys of Andorra"; and the favourite of several derivations of the name Andorra is that which connects it with the biblical En-dor. This origin, if it be the true one, is bound up with the very beginnings of the republic. In 778 Charlemagne marched into Spain against the Moors, drove them towards the Ebro and returned into France through the Pass of Roncesvalles immortalized in the Song of Roland. Somewhat later, he sent his son Louis the Debonair, always known in Andorra as Louis the Pious, into Catalonia to remove once and for all the Moorish threat to Provence. One of the Moorish advanced strongholds was the Spanish

town of Urgel, destined to play henceforth an outstanding part in the history of the republic; and Louis
determined to expel the Moors from Urgel and to
restore the fugitive Christian population. Where now
stands the little capital of the republic, Andorra la

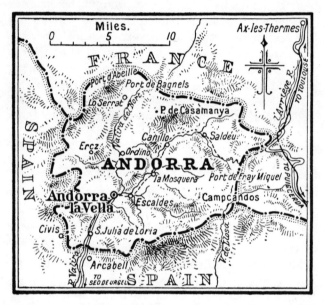

Vella, he utterly broke the Moors, who fled to the south,
never again to enter the valley. The pious king knew
his Old Testament history and his Scripture geography.
Whether he saw in his triumph over the paynim a
resemblance to the battle of Armageddon, where the
true believers overthrew the hosts of heathendom, or
whether it was that the wild valley in which he found

58

himself suggested the witch's cave, he called the place En-dor, now lengthened into Andorra. In the archives of the Cathedral of Urgel there is a charter, dated 819, which purports to grant the Imperial franchise to the valley after this victory. It is now undisputed that this document is a forgery of the eleventh or twelfth century, but there is no doubt that something was done, either by Charlemagne or by his son, by way of enfranchising this and neighbouring Pyrenean valleys. They created a sort of Pyrenean march in order that there might be a wall of Christians as well as of mountains between themselves and the Moors, and they therefore conferred upon the settlers whom they established therein the *jus apusionis*—in other words, some sort of squatter's rights. Of these little marcher states Andorra has long been the sole survivor. There exists, however, an authentic document of 843, whereby Louis's son, Charles the Bald, nominated the Count of Urgel as overlord of Andorra. The *droit Carlovingien*, the tribute due to the Emperor, was now to be paid to the Count of Urgel; and he, for his part, undertook to protect the Andorrans against outside interference.

Three causes have contributed to the preservation of Andorran independence: poverty, inaccessibility and the circumstance that the suzerainty originally exercised by the Count of Urgel alone had soon to be shared with another claimant and has continued to be thus divided to the present day. It was the Bishop of Urgel who disputed the sole suzerainty with the Count. That the

59

valleys of Andorra lay within the Bishop's spiritual jurisdiction was unquestioned, but he now claimed that the Act of consecration of his cathedral, rebuilt in the first half of the ninth century, likewise made them a part of the cathedral's actual endowments. For four centuries the dispute between the lay and the spiritual authorities was waged with great bitterness, and in the meantime the Counts of Foix had become, by marriage, the heirs of the Counts of Urgel. In 1278, through the mediation of the Bishop of Valencia, there was drawn up the "Acte de Paréage," which is the basis of the political and international status of Andorra at the present day. By this compromise the Bishop of Urgel admitted the rights of the Count of Foix to a part in the revenues and overlordship of Andorra and also admitted his right to be represented in the valleys by a deputy, still known as the "*viguier*," from the Latin *vicarius*. It is apparent from the "Acte" that the Bishop already had a similar deputy of his own. Farther, both Count and Bishop were to be represented in the valley by a "*bayle*" (Low Latin *bajulivus*, English "bailiff"), who were jointly to administer justice, while the two suzerains were to levy a tribute on the republic in alternate years. In 1589 Henry II of Foix, who was also Henry III of Navarre, became Henry IV of France, and from that date onwards the lay half of the suzerain rights over Andorra has been exercised by the Head of the French State, whether king, emperor or president. Andorra possesses only one work of art, a Corot presented to the little chapel of its Government building by President Faure, with the following dedication:

"Given in the year 1895 by the President of the French Republic, co-prince of Andorra, in testimony of his sentiments of willing protection and friendship toward the population of the valley."

Félix Faure, with his proper appreciation of the value of wise ceremonial, which his critics denounced as regal proclivities, was an exception to the ordinary run of French presidents, whose tastes and mode of life have generally been far from suggesting the "co-prince" and feudal overlord. Yet these embodiments of a sober and anything but glittering bourgeoisie still very definitely retain the rights that have come to them by political descent from the Counts of Foix; Monsieur Lebrun is still the partner of the Bishop of Urgel in this oddly yoked team. And it is in the main just because of this division of suzerainty that Andorra is an independent entity to-day. In former centuries neither the Count nor the Bishop would allow his rival to dominate the valleys; in modern times neither France nor Spain would tolerate the annexation of Andorra by the other. It has been well remarked that it is impossible to have two masters but not impossible to have two defenders. Had Andorra possessed one overlord only, it would inevitably have been absorbed by the protector. The possession of two has been not only a gain, it has been the cause of its survival.

The Andorrans saw this point clearly enough during the French Revolution, one of the few periods in their long history when their neutrality, and hence their existence, was in serious jeopardy. The regicide Government of 1793 refused to accept the Andorran tribute hitherto paid to the French Crown on the ground that such payments smacked of the hated feudal system. The Andorrans realized the danger to their independence latent in the removal of the French counterweight to the Spanish Bishop's rights; and the world would have witnessed, had it been aware of the circumstance, the unusual if not unique spectacle of one country pleading to be allowed to pay tribute to another. It was not until 1806 that, by order of Napoleon, the relationship of the republic to the Head of the French State was restored. In the meantime the Andorrans had had to take a decision that can only be compared with that taken by Belgium in 1914. In 1794 Spain and revolutionary France were at war and a French army was sent to capture Urgel. The French commander, General Chabert, demanded permission to take his troops through Andorra, only to meet with an uncompromising refusal. Not only did the Council of the Valley protest to Chabert himself as well as to Paris; they mobilized—for the first time, it is believed, for about a thousand years—their entire army, composed of the head of every household and consisting of some five hundred rudely armed but determined men. The French General, although he did not doubt his ability to force his way through the republic, was also not un-mindful of the inconvenience of having a valleyfull of hostile mountaineers on his flank, and chose another route for his march on Urgel.

The republic of Andorra lies about sixty miles from the Mediterranean end of the Pyrenees, and its 191 square miles of territory lie mostly on the Spanish side of the watershed, while its five thousand inhabitants are Catalans by race and Catalan in speech. Of the four miniature states of Europe it is the largest in area, the smallest in population. The Government is in the hands of a General Council of twenty-four members, elected for four years by the heads of families in each of the six parishes and presided over by the Syndic, who is the most important person in the republic. The function of the French and Episcopal *viguiers* is now to preside in the Criminal Court, that of the two *bayles* to act as judges in the Civil Court. There are two Courts of Appeal from the judgments of the *viguiers* and the *bayles*, namely, the Court of the Bishop of Urgel and a special court set up by the French Government at Perpignan to deal with cases from Andorra. Such appeals may be heard in Catalan. The tribute paid to each suzerain is now an annual one of 960 francs to France and 460 pesetas to the Bishop. The French President formerly delegated the actual exercise of his powers to a citizen of the Department of the Ariège, but since 1884 his deputy has been, *ex officio*, the Prefect of the Department of the Pyrénées Orientales. Andorra was late in the field as a stamp-issuing country, resisting the temptation to indulge in its own issues until 1929.

If San Marino is poor and rustic in comparison with states such as Venice and Florence, it is a veritable Venice or Florence in comparison with Andorra. Andorra's villages are constructed of the roughest stone, there is no building that is not of extreme alpine primitiveness, and even the edifice in which its Government has its being—it is known as the "House of the Valley"—is a rough, featureless peasant house. It contains the Council Chamber, a schoolroom, a dining-room and a dormitory for the Councillors when the Council is in session and, in the basement, a stable for their mules. In the Council Chamber is a solid wooden chest heavily bound with iron, in which are the archives of the republic; and it is characteristic of the suspicious temperament of the Andorran that the chest has six locks whose keys are in the charge of the senior Councillors of the six parishes and can only be opened in the presence of them all. There is nothing expansive about the Andorran. He is frugal, he is honest (for smuggling is the national sport of Andorra rather than a moral delinquency), and he is attached to the independence and neutrality of his valley with all the strength of his dour and taciturn temperament. So George Sand was both right and wrong about him. That he is not wanting in the highest degree of courage is proved by his action in 1794; that he lacks the chivalry displayed by the Sammarinesi in their dealings with Garibaldi is perhaps equally true. But no one can refuse their respect to a handful of five thousand people, who have maintained unchanged into this changing epoch a heritage acquired in the Dark Ages.

II

Let us now pass from republics to monarchies and from the largest of the quartet to the smallest, namely, to the four square miles of the Principality of Monaco, the most exiguous piece of territory, I should imagine, with the exception of the Vatican City, that has ever supported the burden of sovereignty.

From the end of the thirteenth century the Genoese family of Grimaldi had been powerful on the Riviera, and by the middle of the fourteenth century Charles I Grimaldi had profited by the struggles between Guelphs and Ghibellines sufficiently to establish himself in the stronghold of Monaco. From that time onwards, despite occasional setbacks, the Grimaldis became gradually more secure in their hold over their lordship; and in 1489 Monaco's independence of any suzerain is admitted by the Duke of Savoy in favour of Lambert Grimaldi, in 1512 in favour of Lucien Grimaldi by the King of France, Lucien being the first Lord of Monaco to exercise the right of coinage. Finally, in 1619, Honoré II Grimaldi discontinues the use of his patronymic in official documents and formally assumes the princely title, being styled hereafter: "Honoré II, Prince et Seigneur de Monaco." His descendant, Louis II, the present Prince of Monaco, is thus the head of one of the oldest dynasties that still occupies a European throne.

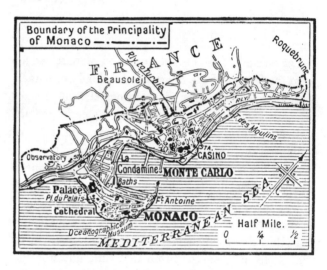

It must not be thought that the reigns of the Lords and Princes of Monaco have been uneventful during these six hundred odd years. Despite the smallness of their domain they have been beset by many troubles—political, dynastic and even matrimonial. In the earlier centuries an object of the conflicting ambitions of Guelphs, Ghibellines and Genoese, then of France and Spain, and well into the nineteenth century of France and Sardinia, the Principality of Monaco has not been

66

able, as have San Marino and Andorra, to "escape notice." She has often been in peril, and to her Princes' motto: "*Deo juvante*," might appropriately have added that of the City of Paris: "*Fluctuat nec mergitur.*" For this miniature monarchy must be to a remarkable extent what the French call *viable;* and, although it was sucked into the vortex of the French Revolution and became in 1793 a part of the French Department of the Alpes Maritimes, yet in 1814 Honoré IV, son of the deposed Prince Honoré III, was able to resume the inheritance, tiny but tenacious, of his ancestors. Thanks to the fact that the younger son of Honoré III, Joseph, had a friend in Talleyrand, the following phrase was added, as if by an afterthought, to paragraph 8 of the first article of the Treaty of Paris by the all-powerful Prince of Benevento: "*Et le Prince de Monaco rentrera dans ses Etats.*"

A pleasing incident is remembered by the Monegasques in connexion with this restoration. In the spring of 1815 the Hereditary Prince, afterwards Prince Regnant as Honoré V (his father, Honoré IV, was too ill personally to assume the reins of government), was on his way to take charge of the Principality. He had served in the French army during the Napoleonic wars, had been Equerry to Napoleon and Grand Equerry to Josephine, had actually been created a Baron of the Empire and was therefore well known to the Imperial family. Shortly after he left Cannes on the night of the 1st March, on his way to Monaco, his coach was suddenly stopped by a body of armed men, at the head of whom Honoré recognized General Cambronne. He was asked to alight and to follow the General to an olive grove, where, sitting at a camp fire, was none other than the Emperor. It was the return from Elba.

"Well, Monaco," said Napoleon; "where are you going?"

"I'm going home, to Monaco," replied the Prince. "And you, Sire?"

"I am going home too, to the Tuileries," laughed Napoleon, adding, according to one version of the story, that, as he would have to take "his cousin's" throne from him, he would keep his Equerry's post open for him at Court.

A reference to the *Almanach de Gotha* will show the Prince of Monaco to be the possessor of an astonishing number of titles. He is Duke of Valentinois, Marquis des Baux, Count of Carladès, Count of Thorigni, Duke of Estouteville, of La Meilleraye and Mayenne, Prince of Château-Porcien, Marquis of Guiscard and the holder of a host of lesser dignities. The well-known boast of the Habsburgs:

Bella gerant alii, tu, felix Austria, nube,

might almost equally well be applied to the Grimaldis for, with the titles accruing from a succession of important marriages, there went the no less important estates from which, until the French Revolution, the Princes

68

derived the greater part of their wealth. Among the peerages that were accumulated in this way by the Grimaldis is also the Duchy of Mazarin, and it is a peculiar coincidence that a Duc de Mazarin in the person of the late Prince of Monaco, Albert I, should have married a Duchesse de Richelieu. There is, however, another side to the picture. Thus Louis I, Prince of Monaco, a godson of Louis XIV, was married to one of the most conspicuous ladies in Europe, the celebrated Charlotte de Gramont, but can have derived little satisfaction from his alliance with this brilliant but flighty lady, who was to form the subject of one of the longest works of Dumas Père.[1] His son, Antony I, married a Princess of Lorraine, but fared little better with her; Antony's grandson, Honoré III, led a miserable existence with his wife, Marie Catherine de Brignole, although it was a love match and the bride was one of the richest heiresses of Genoa. The marriage, indeed, was nearly wrecked at the last moment on the shoals of etiquette. The bride came from Genoa in a galley; her mother insisted that the bridegroom should proceed on board to fetch her; her groom refused, as a Sovereign, to advance farther than the landing-stage. Since neither party would give way the Genoese flotilla withdrew to Bordighera, and only returned two days later because the bride's uncle had in the meantime devised a bridge of boats on which the young couple could meet half-way. Marie Catherine was the heroine of one of the most enduring affections

[1] *Princesse de Monaco.*

recorded in history—although its object was not her husband. Not long after her marriage she became the mistress of Louis Joseph, Prince of Condé, the anti-revolutionary general, and actually married him in 1808, when the liaison had already lasted for forty-eight years and she was seventy and he was seventy-two. They were married in England, where they lived till her death in 1813. How different was the experience of the wife of Honoré IV, the Duchesse de Mazarin in her own right, who, after divorcing Honoré during the French Revolution, was subsequently re-married about half a dozen times, it being stated that four or five of her ex-husbands were finally alive at the same time.

The circumstances which, in the eighteen-sixties, transformed "a rock and an orangery," as the domain of the Lords of Monaco had been called, into the pleasure-ground of Europe, are too well known to need recalling here. Less well known, and perhaps more interesting, are the contacts with England that run in a curiously persistent streak through Monaco's long history. They begin in the Hundred Years' War, when Charles I Grimaldi, commanding one of the fleets of Philip VI of France, raided Southampton in 1339, and are resumed seven years later, when the same Charles, on this occasion the leader of a corps of Genoese cross-bowmen, was left for dead on the battlefield of Crécy. Charles's son Rainer continued in the footsteps of his father and, after the rupture of the Treaty of Bretigni in 1369, fought for the French King Charles V against the English in the north of France, and was actually wrecked off the Isle of Wight in 1372. English affairs next became intertwined with those of Monaco during the Commonwealth, when the Duke of York, afterwards James II, thought of making the harbour of Monaco the base for a Royalist fleet to be organized against Cromwell, and for this purpose entered into negotiations with Honoré II. Of a different character were the English experiences of Honoré's grandson and successor, Louis I. We have seen that this Prince lived on bad terms with his wife, Charlotte de Gramont, a state of affairs by no means due solely to the Princess. Louis embarked upon a spectacular love affair with the beautiful Hortense Mancini, another Duchesse de Mazarin, the great Cardinal's niece, whom it was at one time proposed to marry to Charles II. In 1677 Hortense was living in London on a pension of £4,000 a year from Charles, a power in English politics and the rival of Louise de Quérouailles, the "Madam Carwell" of the popular parlance of the day. Louis followed his lady-love to England and became her acknowledged lover. Charles resented the Monegasque's intrusion and withdrew the lady's pension; Louis, elated beyond measure at his triumph over so powerful a king and so successful a lover, paid it himself—until the lady cast him off for someone better.

English intervention of another sort came after the Treaty of Utrecht, when Queen Anne and Louis XIV were the arbitrators in the matter of the claim of the

Duke of Savoy against the Prince of Monaco, Antony I, to the suzerainty over Mentone and Roquebrune. In 1767 a later Duke of York, Edward, brother of George III, fell suddenly ill while travelling by sea from Marseilles to Genoa and was taken ashore at Monaco, where he died eleven days later in the Prince's palace. The room in the palace in which he died is still called the "York Chamber." Honoré III had done all that was possible for his unexpected guest; George III was duly grateful and sent him six fine horses for his stud, together with an invitation to visit the Court of S. James's. The invitation was accepted and in 1768 Honoré went to England on an official visit of two months, being received in a manner which afforded him the utmost gratification. Less gratifying to Monaco was England's next intervention in its affairs, for it consisted of the occupation of the Principality during the Hundred Days by British troops under a Colonel Burke, representing the Anglo-Sardinian army stationed at Nice and the interests of the Holy Alliance, an occupation which not even the Hereditary Prince's early knowledge of Napoleon's escape from Elba was able to prevent. And the latest association of Great Britain with Monaco was the first marriage of the late Prince Albert I, the oceanographer, to the daughter of the eleventh Duke of Hamilton, of which marriage the present Prince is the only issue. There is thus a relationship between King George V and Prince Louis II, albeit a distant one; both are descended from Henry VII. Perhaps one more English contact may be mentioned, if a somewhat indirect one. Monaco's name had already been borrowed for the purposes of political satire when Victorien Sardou staged his play "Rabagas" in the Principality. Similarly, in 1874, there was published in London by Macmillans a book entitled *The Fall of Prince Florestan of Monaco*, by "Himself." This work seeks to describe the internal conflict of a man, of princely birth but of republican ideas, succeeding to a throne which purports to be that of Monaco. The book is, in point of fact, a political skit written by the late Sir Charles Dilke.

The rulers of Monaco began, as we have seen, to strike coins in the reign of Lucien early in the sixteenth century, and under several of the subsequent princes there was a considerable output from the Monaco mint. But what a *dégringolade* has there been in this respect in these hard post-War times. Prince Charles III and Prince Albert coined only gold—the latter, indeed, nothing smaller than a piece of one hundred francs (pre-War), whose intrinsic value was £4. Prince Louis II has struck nothing—hitherto, at all events—but humble francs and fifty-centimes pieces of billon. The postage stamps of the Principality, on the other hand, which began under Charles III in 1885, become annually more numerous and more magnificent. It was under Charles III that the Principality was reduced to its present small extent by the cession to France, in

1861, of the towns of Mentone and Roquebrune, which in point of fact had thrown off their allegiance to the Grimaldis in 1848. But it was the same sagacious Prince who, two years after this loss, restored the fortunes of what remained of his domain by granting to Monsieur Louis Blanc the concession which soon made Prince, Principality and Monsieur Blanc extremely affluent.

The Principality of Liechtenstein, which is bounded on the east by the Austrian province of Vorarlberg, on the west by the Rhine and the Swiss Canton of St. Gall, on the south by the Canton of Grisons, has an area of sixty-five square miles and a population of about eleven thousand and is one of the rare examples of a state that has adopted the name of its rulers. Territorially it is composed of two former fiefs of the Holy Roman Empire—the County of Vaduz and the Lordship of Schellenberg—the former comprising, roughly speaking, the mountains and the southern section of the Rhine Valley, the latter the low-lying northern part of the Principality. In the twelfth century the property of the Counts of Montfort, these fiefs then passed in succession to the Barons of Brandis, the Counts of Sulz and the Counts of Hohenems, in whose possession they remained until James Hannibal III of Hohenems, yielding to the pressure of his creditors, sold Schellenberg in 1699 to Prince John Adam of Liechtenstein, the head of an Austrian noble family unconnected with the territory that was soon to bear his name. Thirteen years later John Adam realized the ambition of his House to become princes in fact as well as in title by means of the ownership of an immediate fief of the Roman Em-

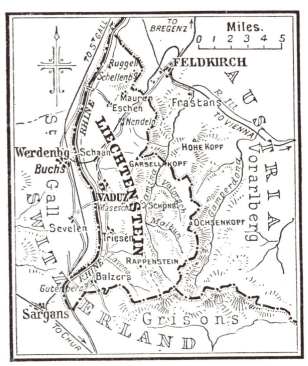

pire and reception into the Imperial College of Princes by purchasing Vaduz also from James Hannibal. Imperial confirmation was given to these proceedings in 1719, when the Emperor Charles VI raised Vaduz and Schellenberg into an hereditary State of the Holy

Roman Empire, giving it the name of its new owners, the Principality of Liechtenstein.

Throughout Liechtenstein there is ample evidence of the Principality's sovereign status. In the parish church of Vaduz, the royal pew above the choir is surmounted by Liechtenstein's complicated coat of arms in stone; the same coat of arms in mosaic adorns the façade of the Government building. Throughout the land the national colours of blue and red are to be seen beside the dynastic colours of red and white. Motor-vehicles plying in the Principality bear on the number-plate a blue and red shield with the letters F.L. (Fürstenthum Liechtenstein). Liechtenstein has its own postage stamps and shares the tendency of most small states to indulge in frequent changes of design, but with consistent æsthetic success. Its coins, which, while legal tender only within the Principality, are also current in Swiss frontier towns such as Sargans and Buchs, are among the handsomest coins of the twentieth century.

The present Prince, Francis I, who succeeded his brother John II in 1929, is the eleventh of his House to reign in Liechtenstein, and several of his predecessors have been men of distinction, even of fame, although none of them visited his Principality until 1842. Outstanding among the earlier princes was Joseph Wenzel, one of Maria Theresa's Field-Marshals in the Seven Years' War; Aloysius I was a noted patron of the arts; John I, who reigned from 1805 to 1836, was an Austrian Field-Marshal in the Napoleonic wars, and in 1809 succeeded the Archduke Charles in the supreme command of the Imperial forces. The late Prince, John II, had the remarkable experience of entering upon the seventy-first year of a minority-less reign—an event without parallel in the history of modern Europe—having ascended the throne of his miniature Principality in 1858, when in his nineteenth year, and surviving until 1929.[1] During his unprecedentedly long reign Liechtenstein experienced some remarkable vicissitudes, both in its own affairs and in those of its neighbours. At the time of Prince John's accession a member of the Germanic Confederation, the Principality took part in an unsuccessful war against Prussia, saw the break-up of the Confederation, entered into economic union first with Austria, then with Switzerland, and witnessed the disappearance in this period of the five empires of continental Europe—the French, the Russian, the German, the Austrian and the Ottoman. The singular range of his reign was reflected in Prince John's coinage. In 1862 he struck "*Vereinthalers*" in common with the other members of the Germanic Confederation; at the end of the nineteenth century and the beginning of the twentieth there appeared a handsome series of gold and silver coins in Austrian crown currency, bearing on the obverse the Prince's effigy and on the reverse his arms encircled by the Collar of the Golden Fleece. At the end of his reign, after the disappearance of the Austrian Empire,

[1] See the note on p. 113.

77

the same prince issued coins of the same general design, with the difference that the Swiss franc took the place of the Austrian crown. That this tiny state should have weathered the storms that shattered powerful neighbours and should have remained, to the pride of its inhabitants, the sole surviving monarchy not only of German-speaking lands but of Central Europe, is due not altogether to its political insignificance; it is due in no small measure to the devotion which the dynasty has been able to inspire in its inhabitants.

Liechtenstein is wholly Catholic in religion and is now wholly German-speaking; but many Romansch place-names such as Valors, Garsella, Masescha, Lavena, Samina, Malbun, attest the Rhætian origin of its people. Ecclesiastically, indeed, it forms to the present day a part of the diocese of Chur (*Curia Rhætorum*). It is a happy little pastoral and agricultural country, producing fine cattle in its lovely alpine valleys and delicious table wines in its vineyards along the Rhine. In 1868, after the Austro-Prussian War, Liechtenstein abolished compulsory military service; and partly on this account, partly because of its favoured position in all other respects, taxation is light and the cost of living low. This circumstance explains why few Liechtensteiners emigrate; it also explains why, since the Great War, a small but growing number of North German "tax-dodgers" has been finding its way to this beautiful and sheltered corner of Europe, not altogether to the joy of its inhabitants. Although there is no truth in the

PLATE III

The Reigning Prince (Francis I) and Princess of Liechtenstein.

Vaduz and its Castle.   Vaduz : Government Offices and
Church.

A Street in Yvetot.   *To face p. 78.*

oft-repeated assertion that Liechtenstein is still in a state of war with Prussia (for Liechtenstein was a party to the Treaty of Prague), Prussian immigration meets with little sympathy from the Liechtensteiners, who, while they look back with kindly thoughts on the Austrian connexion, have not yet developed a liking for the people against whom they fought their last campaign. "Liechtenstein for the Liechtensteiners" is their prevailing sentiment; and, although since 1920 a very few have begun to talk of the possible advantages of union with Switzerland, the idea has found no real support.

With a rich soil and a good climate, relieved from international anxieties, with a prosperous and contented population, with no industrial problems or large towns (Vaduz, the capital, has only about twelve hundred inhabitants), with wealthy and beneficent rulers who gladly place their private resources at the disposal of their people, the Principality of Liechtenstein is indeed an alpine Arcadia, a little oasis of peace and happiness in this disturbed modern world of ours. It is not to be wondered at that the politics of the great majority of Liechtensteiners are summed up in the formula: "bourgeois, Catholic, dynastic."

III

Article 3 of the Lateran Treaty of 1929, in creating the Vatican City as an independent State under the sovereignty of the Holy See, brought into existence a political organism such as the world has not previously seen, for never before in the history of mankind have the attributes of sovereignty, as exemplified in Courts of Law, prisons, passports, coins and postage stamps, rested on a territorial basis of 108 acres, supporting a

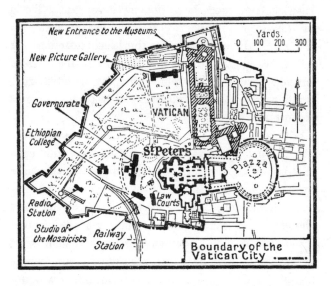

population of 639, of whom only two are native-born. Never before has there been an independent country with only 42 street-names; never before one whose maps are scaled not to miles but to yards. The fact of the matter is that the State of the Vatican City belongs not so much to geography as to history. Its acres are the consequence rather than the cause of the sovereignty of the Holy See.

80

Approximately one quarter of the area of the State is occupied by S. Peter's Church, a quarter by the Vatican and the remainder by the Papal gardens and by the administrative buildings with which Pius XI is rapidly covering the inclines behind the apse of S. Peter's. Tiny as is his temporal dominion, it is politically complete, has even its railway and broadcasting stations, has its own number-plate for motor-cars, a red shield with the letters S.C.V. (Stato Città Vaticana). These things, and the other manifestations of political rule, necessitate an administrative apparatus to which its scanty acres bear no relation; and that is why a large Governorate, why Courts of Law, departmental buildings and a prison have arisen, almost mushroom-like, in the last few years on the Vatican Hill. Anomalies there are in plenty in this latest reconstruction of the States of the Church, not one of the least piquant being that it contains a greater proportion of military to civil inhabitants than any other country in the world. What with the Noble Guard, the Swiss Guard, the Palatine Guard and the Pontifical Gendarmerie, about one half of the population of the State must be uniformed and armed.

The Vatican City suggests another organization which, although it has no longer any territorial basis, yet retains even now its theoretical independence and continues to exercise some, at all events, of the attributes of political sovereignty. When the Sovereign Order of S. John of Jerusalem lost Malta in 1798, it did not at the same time lose its independent status. No lands now remained under the political rule of the Knights, who transferred the seat of the Grand Master first to Catania in Sicily, then to Ferrara and, finally, to Rome. But even now, in this drab post-War period, His Most Eminent Highness Prince Chigi della Rovere Albani, seventy-sixth Grand Master in succession from the Blessed Raymond du Puy, sends and receives Diplomatic Envoys to and from other Courts, and issues passports to officials and members of the Grand Magistracy of the Order.

The tail-piece of this chapter shall be a "freak of freedom" in the most literal sense of the words: the district of Moresnet. This little State, which lay on the borders of Belgium and Rhenish Prussia, was between 1815 and 1919 the most perfect example of a political no-man's-land ever known. Embracing an area of 1,400 acres and having a population of 3,000, it owed its origin to the failure of the Congress of Vienna to come to a decision as to its ownership. As no agreement could be reached between rival claimants and as the Congress was not prepared to prolong its sittings for so trifling a territory, it was made a separate State under the joint government of Prussia and the Netherlands, which then included what is now the Kingdom of Belgium. This arrangement endured until 1841, when Moresnet was given its own administration of a burgomaster and a Council of 10 members, the inhabitants being allowed to decide for themselves whether they would perform military service for Belgium or for Prussia and would accept the jurisdiction of the Prussian or the Belgian Courts. It was not until after the Great War, when the neighbouring districts of Eupen

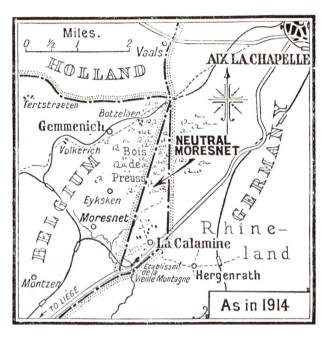

and Malmédy were transferred to Belgium, that Moresnet's independent status came to an end. Possessing valuable woods, it was assigned to Belgium "in partial compensation for the destruction of Belgian forests" by the German armies during the War.

IL ÉTAIT UN
ROI D'YVETOT

IL ÉTAIT UN ROI D'YVETOT

Il était un roi d'Yvetot
  Peu connu dans l'histoire,
Se levant tard, se couchant tôt,
  Dormant fort bien sans gloire,
Et couronné par Jeanneton
D'un simple bonnet de coton,
     Dit-on.
Oh! Oh! Oh! Oh! Ah! Ah! Ah! Ah!
Quel bon petit roi c'était là!
    La! La!

Il n'agrandit point ses Etats,
  Fut un voisin commode,
Et, modèle des potentats,
  Prit le plaisir pour code.
Ce n'est que lorsqu'il expira
Que le peuple qui l'enterra
    pleura.
Oh! Oh! Oh! Oh! Ah! Ah! Ah! Ah!
Quel bon petit roi c'était là!
    La! La!

IN 1813, when the glories of the First Empire were already on the wane, Béranger, then beginning to emerge from ill-health and the direst misery, wrote the most famous of his songs as a satire on Napoleon. Robert Louis Stevenson has said of Béranger that he

was the only poet of modern times who could altogether
have dispensed with printing, for his songs were learned
by heart and passed from one convivial gathering in
France to another. Béranger's concern in writing the
song was, as I have said, with the great Emperor; in so
far as he and his audiences were interested in the
ostensible subject-matter, the King of Yvetot, it was
only to smile at what was to them but a legendary *roi
pour rire*. It is the object of the following pages to show
· that not only once *il était un roi d'Yvetot*, but a succession of such kings; and that for nearly two centuries the
lords of this Norman fief bore, and bore with right, the
royal style.

Almost equidistant from Rouen, Havre and Dieppe,
the little town of Yvetot in the Pays de Caux figures in
the lists of Norman feudal holdings as early as the
eleventh century. John, Lord of Yvetot, is recorded to
have been among the Norman seigneurs who took part
in the Battle of Hastings; in 1147 Gaultier d'Yvetot is
mentioned in attendance on Henry Plantagenet, afterwards our King Henry II, and appears to have taken the
cross; in 1206 Robert d'Yvetot was bound to provide
King Philip Augustus with one-third of the equipment
of a man-at-arms: *Robertus de Yvetot tertiam partem
militis.* So far, there was nothing to distinguish Yvetot
from other fiefs; indeed, Robert's obligation to contribute to the upkeep of a man-at-arms proves that Yvetot
was at that time certainly not free from the ordinary
feudal obligations. The change of status seems to have

come towards the end of the fourteenth century, when John IV of Yvetot, who was *maistre d'Hostel* to, and high in the favour of the French King Charles V, was suddenly distinguished with the style and title of King. The official document in which this attribution appears for the first time is a decree of the Norman Court of Exchequer of the year 1392.

What exactly does this application of the dignity of king to a simple fief, and a small one at that, imply? It implies that the fief had become what was sometimes called a *franc fief*, that its lord had unlimited legal jurisdiction over his dependents, that he had no obligation to provide the King of France with fighting men or himself to follow him in the field, that he was exempt from the payment of tribute, that in the case of a minority the King of France had not the right of guardianship. When Yvetot became possessed of these privileges is not clear; it may have been at the time when the Spanish merchants who unloaded their merchandise at Harfleur used Yvetot as an entrepôt where they bartered their goods to the merchants of France and thus enabled the Lord of Yvetot to exact customs dues on the transactions. In the twelfth century the Lords of Yvetot imposed a toll on those crossing the Seine between Pontaudemer and Caudebec, and in 1203 they sold this right to the Abbey of S. Wandrille, *excepto passagio sibi et hominibus ipsius, de libero feodo de Yvetot*. More than a decade before the judgment of the Court of Exchequer the Lords of Yvetot were describing themselves as holding their lordship "by the grace of God"; in a deed dated the 11th January, 1381, John IV signs himself *"sire d'Yvetot par la grâce de Dieu."* From various charters and documents of the Court of France it is established that the Lords of Yvetot imposed on their subjects the tax known as the *quatrième*, a right confined to the King of France in the case of fiefs not entirely free; that they had the right of coinage and of pardon; that they enjoyed, and retained until 1553, the privilege of final legal jurisdiction in the sense that their decisions were not subject to appeal to the French Courts. For the rest, although there has not been found any charter converting Yvetot from an ordinary fief into a kingdom, there is a succession of French official acts in which the seigneurs of the place are referred to as Kings of Yvetot; and, as recently as 1543, Letters Patent of King Francis I describe the Lady of Yvetot as Queen. Even Louis XI, that determined centralizer and exterminator of the great feudatories, confirmed the privileges of the King of Yvetot, granting him *"de jouir doresnavant de toutes et chacunes des franchises, libertés, droitures, prérogatives et prééminences dont il apparaissait que les précédents seigneurs d'Yvetot jouissaient au tems auparavant la descente des Anglais à Touques."* It is related of Louis that, finding himself one day on the soil of the pigmy kingdom, he turned with a smile to his following and said: "My Lords, there is no longer a king in France."

Indeed, although Yvetot was described by Voltaire

as *"un royaume infiniment petit et presque honteux,"* and is probably the smallest unit ever to have sustained the kingly title, we must not forget that the Kings of Aragon created the kingdoms of Majorca and Minorca for their younger sons and that there is the example nearer home of the Isle of Man, probably the closest parallel to Yvetot that can be found in modern times. A French poet of the sixteenth century wrote as follows:—

> "Au noble païs de Caux
> Y a quatre abbaïes royaux;
> Six prieurez conventuaux,
> Et six barons de grand arroi,
> Quatre comtes, trois ducs, un roi."

Few kingdoms have seen a greater number of dynasties in occupation of their throne. John IV was succeeded by Martin I, who exercised his right of coinage and is commemorated by a medal in which he appears seated on a mediæval *banc royal*, with a circlet on his head, giving the accolade to one of his subjects named Bobé. Unfortunately King Martin I found himself obliged to sell his kingdom, the purchaser being one Peter de Vilaines, Chamberlain of the French King Charles VI, who took the name of Peter I. This Peter I was succeeded by his son, Peter II, who died during the English invasion after seeing his capital burned to the ground. For in 1407 the English landed at Touques and made themselves masters of Normandy, including the domain of the unfortunate Peter. This occupation led to the one English intervention in the affairs of our little kingdom, for Henry V granted to John Holland, Mayor of Bordeaux, the sum of 800 livres to be found by the land of Yvetot, which he was to hold from the King in fief. The fortunes of war did not allow John Holland a long enjoyment of his realm. To him succeeded one Guillaume Chenu, the collateral heir of the House of Vilaines, who endowed his subjects with a large well and struck a medal with the inscription: *Haurite Aquas cum Gaudio de Puteo.*

From the family of Chenu the throne of Yvetot passed by marriage to that of Baucher in the person of John Baucher, Councillor and Chamberlain of the King of France. This Baucher was a personage of a certain importance, who deserves to be remembered if only by reason of the remarkable letter which he wrote to the sister of King Charles VIII, Anne de Beaujeu, who at the time was exercising the Regency. Anne had lost her son in early youth and was troubled at the absence of an heir. The King of Yvetot proffered his advice to the Regent of France how to replace the lamented heir with a frankness that leaves nothing to be desired:—

"MADAME,

J'envoye ce pourteur en court devers le Roy mon Seigneur et vous prie vous remonstrer les afayres de mon Royaume, auquel, si vous ne mectez la main, par ma foy, ils sont bien au bas.

Madame, je vous avertis que si vous recommandez à Nostre Dame de Haulte Faye, en Agenais, au plaisir de Dieu et de Nostre-Dame, vous serez bien tost grosse, car toutes les faimes qui s'y recommandent ne faillent point, ainsi que on m'a dict.

Madame, je vous supplie m'avoir toujours pour vostre loyal serviteur.

Madame, je prie à Dieu et à Nostre-Dame-de-Haulte-Faye que vous doint bonne vie et longue.

Escript à Dinan le XVe jour de Janvier, 1490.

Vostre très humble et très obéissant serviteur,

LE ROY D'YVETOT."

It is satisfactory to recall that on the 10th May, 1491, Anne de Beaujeu gave birth to a daughter.

John Baucher died in 1500, his death being recorded in the Chronicle of Monstrelet in the following terms: "*Le jour Saint-Anne, XXVIe jour de juillet, trespassa à Lyon le Roy d'Yvetot et fust enterré à Sainte-Croix, près Saint-Jean-de-Lyon;*" and the rights over Yvetot returned to the House of Chenu. First came James Chenu, then his brother Peter or Pérot, who, on the occasion of Charles VIII's formal entry into Paris, took part in the procession wearing a royal crown. It may have been the convivial and democratic habits attributed to this monarch that inspired the song of Béranger. With Pérot's son John ended the male line of Chenu, for John left only a daughter, married to an important nobleman of Anjou, Martin du Bellay, who became King of Yvetot *jure uxoris*. Martin du Bellay had been an ambassador, was a favourite of Francis I, and became his Governor of Normandy. These important duties did not, however prevent him from devoting himself to his little kingdom, and he sought from Francis and his successor, Henry II, confirmation of its special privileges. But the Parliament of Normandy had always been jealous of these; and, when Henry II's Letters Patent were sent to that body for registration, the Normans submitted "very humble remonstrances to His Majesty anent the danger of having within the kingdom of France another kingdom with sovereign rights", and urged that the maintenance of the privileges of Yvetot would be a shocking abuse which should be done away with.

Despite Martin's efforts, he was unable to prevail against the deputation which the Norman Parliament sent to the King with its representations, with the result that, while the lordship of Yvetot continued to be free of fiscal charges, its right of the high justice was withdrawn. And so from 1555 onwards the Lords of Yvetot had to abandon the title of King for that of Prince; and when, at the coronation of Marie de' Medici in 1610, Henry IV noticed that the Lord of Yvetot of the time, another Martin du Bellay, had not been suitably accommodated, it was in kindly jest rather than in literal earnest that he said: *"Je veux que l'on donne une place honorable à mon petit roi d'Yvetot, selon la qualité et le rang qu'il doit tenir."* The male line of the du Bellays came to an end in the second half of the seventeenth century and Yvetot passed by a series of marriages to the family of Crévant and from them to that of d'Albon.

The family of d'Albon was one of the oldest noble Houses of France, the Counts d'Albon having been established at Grenoble from the time of Charles Martel. In the first half of the twelfth century Guigues IV, Count d'Albon, assumed a dolphin for his armorial bearings, and thereafter the head of the family was called the Dauphin and his estate Dauphiné. This circumstance explains the following pleasant episode. One day, in the reign of Louis XIV, the Grand Dauphin of France was crossing the Pont Neuf when he observed a coach emblazoned, like his own, with the arms of Dauphiné. Surprised and indignant, he stopped and sent to ask of the occupant of the coach, who was Camillus I d'Albon, Prince of Yvetot, by what right he was displaying his, the Dauphin's, arms.

"Tell Monseigneur," replied Camillus, "that it is not I who am bearing his arms but he who is bearing mine."

It was this Camillus who in 1711 sought to prevent a farther encroachment on his lordship's privileges by protesting against the imposition of the tax known as the *dixième denier*, which was a tax for the defence of the frontier. Again the decision went against Yvetot, for it was ruled that "since the kingdom of France served as a barrier to protect the Principality of Yvetot, the latter must contribute in accordance with its means for the defence of the frontier, for the enemies of the Crown of France would not respect the said Principality of

Yvetot should they succeed in penetrating into the Pays de Caux." So here was yet another curtailment of the powers enjoyed by John IV and his successors; nevertheless, Camillus I was still addressed in formal documents as *"le Très Haut et Puissant Seigneur, Messire Camille d'Albon, Prince Souverain d'Yvetot."* This Prince was succeeded in 1729 by his relative and son-in-law, Claud d'Albon, who was followed by his son Camillus II. The latter, who was always in financial straits and took no interest in Yvetot, resigned his rights over it in favour of his son on the latter's marriage in 1772; and this son, Camillus III, was the last of the long line of the Lords of Yvetot. Camillus III had literary ambitions, corresponded with Voltaire and the Encyclopædists and published a number of works on history and political science. *Felix opportunitate mortis*, he died in October, 1789, two months after the States-General had decreed the abolition of all privileges throughout France.

With that absence of *pietas* which all too often has characterized post-revolutionary France, the people of Yvetot have done nothing to preserve, have in fact done their best to eradicate the memories of their rulers, who, if not particularly remarkable or heroic, have at all events given to this insignificant Norman town a special place in history. Thus, the parish church of red brick, rebuilt by Camillus II and Camillus III after a fire which destroyed the greater part of the town in 1688, no longer bears on the façade its former inscription:—

DEO VIVENTI
CAMILLUS III.

No public monuments recall the history to which alone
Yvetot owes what fame she possesses in the outer world.
It is true that the Corn Exchange built by Camillus III
still stands between the Place des Belges and the Place
du Maréchal Joffre, although now converted into a theatre
cum cinema *cum* Baths *cum* "salle de réunion"; but
even here the tablet erected by its builder with the
following inscription:—

GENTIUM COMMODO
CAMILLUS III
MDCCLXXXVI

has been removed from the front of the building and
replaced at the back. But I must confess that it was
pleasant to find, even if tucked away more or less out
of sight, the inscription of a separate dynasty, especially
with so sonorous a name as Camillus and set up within
fifteen years of the nineteenth century, still standing on
the soil of France. The visitor seeking visible traces of
Yvetot's past must be persistent and must be prepared
to dispense with the assistance of the local inhabitants.
There is indeed very little for him to find apart from
the Corn Exchange. Despite prolonged search I could
discover nothing but two objects in the parish church.
One is a stained glass window showing John IV, King
of Yvetot, wearing a red robe lined with ermine and a

G   97

royal crown encircling a blue bonnet, presenting the charter of foundation of the Collegiate Church of Yvetot to John de Maugy, Archbishop of Rouen, in 1351. The inscription states that the window was erected in memory of the Venerable M. Guéroult, *"dernier Doyen de la Collegiale d'Yvetot, imprisonné sous la Terreur en 1793 et mort sur les Pontons de Rochefort en 1794 martyr de sa foi."* The second object was a faded and inconspicuous Brief of Pope Pius VI affixed to the back wall of the church, granting a plenary indulgence *"aux instances de Camille d'Albon"* to those confessing in the church on specified days. The church itself is extremely ugly, but the choir-boys are dressed in scarlet cassocks, scarlet capes, scarlet skull-caps, socks and shoes and in white rochets, and look exactly like baby Cardinals.

A gentleman of Yvetot has recently produced on his native town a little book in which, after remarking complacently that nothing remains of its antiquities, he proceeds to work himself up, rather in the manner of the preachers of Italian *fervorini*, to fill several pages with raptures over its modern amenities, over the graces of its flour-mill, the æsthetic charms of its cider distillery. *"Non point,"* he says without a regret, *"qu'Yvetot puisse offrir la moindre curiosité archéologique; tout vestige de son antique passé se trouve aujourd'hui disparu."* On the other hand, *"aussitôt parvenu sur la place de la gare, le touriste, d'un coup d'œil rapide, embrasse le vaste panorama de la ville, aux abords plaisants. A gauche, se*

98

détachant sur des lointains de verdure, s'élèvent les impor-tants bâtiments d'une minoterie moderne et non loin de ceux-ci une jolie maison de maître. Puis c'est un vaste jardin à la française au fond duquel se profile, gracieuse, la tourelle d'une riche villa." He even manages to get a thrill out of the station inn, the most banal little *estaminet* that can be imagined, but to him, as he sees it through his magic glasses, "*accueillant avec sa gaie façade de briques neuves agrémentée de rouges géraniums.*" Can fatuity go farther?

"*Coquet*" and "*cossu*" are this writer's favourite epithets for the modern Yvetot: "*C'est un ensemble de rues très propres tracées sur un sol égal, bordées de coquets jardins, de gentilles maisons d'agrément, d'avenants magasins de commerce, coupées çà et là de vastes places encadrant les principaux edifices de la cité, que parcourt le touriste charmé par l'aspect riant, calme et ordonné de la capitale cauchoise. . . . Mais c'est un ensemble 'cossu' d'importantes constructions qui révèle l'aisance et l'activité de la cité: mentionnons:*" and here follows a list of schools and markets, the post office and what not.

I traverse this gentleman's dithyrambics point blank: *cossu* the little town may be; *coquet* it is emphatically not. On the contrary, it is a dull, dreary little place, and the Yvetotais seem to do their best to prevent it from being anything else. The streets are modern and drab, the new Town Hall is vulgar and ugly. On the other hand, I found two names among its inhabitants which gave me genuine pleasure. One was the delightful patronymic "Gogibu" surmounting the window of a confectioner's shop; the other was the unusual family name "Finance," borne, not inappropriately, perhaps, by the host of the Hôtel des Victoires. This old coaching inn is one of the few buildings in Yvetot of any attractions whatever, and Monsieur Finance certainly put up an excellent luncheon, which began with an admirable home-made *pâté* of hare and was washed down by locally brewed cider.

It is a question whether Béranger did more harm or good to the reputation of little Yvetot by popularizing it in his ballad. He probably made its inhabitants self-conscious, gave them, in the phraseology of our age, an inferiority complex. So, too, I dare say, did Monsieur Adam, whose light opera, "Le Roi d'Yvetot," was one of the most popular items of the repertoire of the Paris Opéra Comique in the middle of the last century. Perhaps, therefore, we cannot take the modern Yvetotais too severely to task if they feel that their history tends to make them faintly ludicrous; if they seek refuge from their embarrassment by emphasizing the charms, not obvious to anyone else, of their mills and their factories and even their station inn.

EUROPE'S LAST
GRAND DUCHY

IV

EUROPE'S LAST GRAND DUCHY

THERE is one European country too large to figure among the four miniature states of Europe, Monaco, San Marino, Liechtenstein and Andorra, yet at the same time considerably smaller in area and population than any other independent European country not forming a part of a greater confederation. With its area of 999 square miles and its population of a little under 300,000, the Grand Duchy of Luxemburg would have made quite a sizable member of some larger entity. Completely independent as it is, it occupies a sort of half-way house—and occupies it alone—between the miniature states of Europe and those of more normal dimensions.

The Empire founded by Charlemagne was great in extent but of short duration. In its entirety it barely survived the death of his successor, Louis the Debonair, whose three sons disputed the inheritance for the three years following their father's death in 840 until, by the Treaty of Verdun, they divided the Empire into three kingdoms. The middle kingdom, forming a long stretch of territory that comprised the modern Belgium, Luxemburg, Eastern France and Northern Italy, fell to the share of the eldest brother, Lothair, from whom a part of it derived its name, becoming first Lotharingia and subsequently Lorraine. The second brother, Louis the German, received the eastern kingdom, which was more or less the present Germany east of the Rhine.

The third kingdom, which included the greater part of France with Flanders, fell to Charles the Bald. Not unnaturally, the central kingdom became the object of almost incessant struggles between the two others, and in a sense the Franco-Prussian War and the Great War of 1914–18 may be said to have been the latest manifestations of this secular contest. It is to its geographical and political situation between the French and the German elements, having much of each race in its blood and speech yet having insufficient strength and extent to serve as an adequate buffer between them, that Luxemburg owes its singularly restless history, while the circumstance that its capital was, until it was dismantled in 1867, one of the strongest fortresses in Europe brought it even more into the orbit of international jealousies and ambitions.

The name Luxemburg is derived from the Teutonic "Lucilin-burhuc," meaning "little fortress"; and it was this stronghold, which is believed to have owed its origin to the Roman Emperor Gallienus and remained formidable for sixteen centuries, that gave its name to the Grand Duchy and to one of the most powerful dynasties of the Middle Ages. The first family to reign in Luxemburg was that of the Counts of Ardenne, who, descended in the female line from Charlemagne, built up around the fortress of Luxemburg one of the many lordships that arose on the ruins of the Carolingian Empire. The male line of the Counts of Ardenne came to an end in 1136, when Luxemburg passed to the Count of Namur, Henry the Blind, sister's son to the last Count of Ardenne. The union of the counties of Namur and Luxemburg, although it was short-lived, was to have an important influence on the subsequent developments of the latter, for the connexion with Namur brought to Luxemburg, hitherto mainly

Germanic in character, important elements of Latin civilization. Henry's daughter, Ermesinde, one of Luxemburg's greatest rulers, married as her second husband Walram of Limburg, and by this marriage there was likewise amalgamated with Luxemburg the marquisate of Arlon. Henceforth the land of Luxemburg contained two distinct and almost equal ethnographic and linguistic elements, the Germanic and the Walloon, until it lost almost all its Walloon districts to Belgium in 1839.

The dynasty founded by Ermesinde and Walram was to make the name of Luxemburg for a time predominant in Central Europe: it was to give three Emperors and two Kings of the Romans to Germany, four Kings to Bohemia, two Electors to Brandenburg and one King to Hungary. The first of the Emperors of this House, Ermesinde's third successor, reigned as Henry V, Count of Luxemburg, from 1288 to 1309 and as Henry VII, Holy Roman Emperor, from 1308 until his death in 1313 in Italy, which he had entered in the last serious effort that was made to revive the Imperial power in the peninsula. Henry's attempt to reduce Italy to the obedience of the Emperor, although it resulted in little more than his coronation in Rome, profoundly affected the imagination of his age, as may be judged by the hopes built upon his arrival by Dante in the *De Monarchia*. And even more enduring has proved the fame of his son and successor in Luxemburg, John, King of Bohemia, the second of Luxemburg's rulers to be called "the Blind." John is not only regarded by the Luxemburgers as the most chivalrous figure in their annals, but has a picturesque niche in English history as well. The story of his death is too familiar to require more than an allusion here. On the outbreak of the Hundred Years' War, John, ever restless and ever in pursuit of knight-errantry, hastened to the assistance of his friend and ally, King Philip VI of France, accompanied by his son Charles and 500 knights of Luxemburg and Bohemia. He had already lost one eye in 1336 on an expedition against the Lithuanians, and four years later bad medical treatment rendered him totally blind. With his little army he took part in the battle of Crécy and, when he was told that the day was lost, led a last forlorn hope with fifty knights, whose horses were attached to his. At night, the victorious English found him and his companions dead on the field of battle; and so moved, according to the well-known story, was the Black Prince by this act of gallantry that he took John's helmet with its three ostrich feathers and adopted thereafter as his own motto that of the fallen king: "Ich dien." Even in death the luckless king did not find rest. His remains were first taken to the Abbey of Altmünster in Luxemburg, where they lay until the Abbey was destroyed during the French Revolution. They were then transferred to a little church in the lower town of Luxemburg, but in the course of time found their way into the hands of vandals, who sold them to a crockery merchant at a village called Mettlach on the Sarre. Here they remained, exhibited as a curiosity in the crockery merchant's shop, until 1838, when Frederick William IV of Prussia removed them and laid them in a porphyry tomb at Castel, overlooking the Sarre, where perhaps they will now be suffered to repose in peace.

John was succeeded in Bohemia by his eldest son Charles, who as the Emperor Charles IV raised Luxemburg from a County to a Duchy in favour of his younger brother Wenceslas. Under the Emperor Charles the House of Luxemburg rose to the summit of its power, its possessions extending from the mouth of the Scheldt to the Eastern Carpathians, while under Duke Wenceslas Luxemburg itself reached its greatest extent, which was four times greater than the area of the Grand Duchy to-day. The family was at this time conspicuous also for its wealthy marriages, and it is of interest to note that another brother of Wenceslas, John of Moravia, was the first husband of Margaret Maultasch, the "Ugly Duchess" of Tyrol. Wenceslas I was succeeded by his nephew of the same name, known as "the Drunkard," who prepared the way for the ruin of his country. Crowned King of the Romans in the lifetime of his father, the Emperor Charles IV, the greatest ruler whom Europe produced in the fourteenth century, he could, had his character resembled that of Charles, have worn after him the Imperial crown. Instead, he frittered away his lands and his wealth and finally pawned Luxemburg to his niece, Elizabeth of

Goerlitz, for 120,000 florins. His brother and successor, the Emperor Sigismund, was the last male of the House of Luxemburg, and died before he was able to redeem the Duchy; and in 1442 Elizabeth of Goerlitz sold her rights over it to her nephew, Philip the Good, Duke of Burgundy. The end of Luxemburg's national dynasty coincided with the loss of its independence. For the ensuing four centuries Luxemburg was to have neither a dynasty of its own nor separate individuality. Its history is now merged in that of the greater states, with which it is united either by force of arms or by the vagaries of international politics and combinations.

Over these four centuries, therefore, it will suffice to cast a very cursory glance. After sixty years of Burgundian rule Luxemburg passed by inheritance to the great Emperor Charles V, who began life as Duke of Luxemburg, with which title he was invested at his birth. After his death it became an appanage of the Spanish Crown, and as such existed miserably until 1714. It then passed, in consequence of the Treaties of Utrecht and Rastadt, to the Emperor Charles VI, head of the Austrian branch of the House of Habsburg, under whom it lived happily enough until the outbreak of the French Revolution. In 1792 Luxemburg was invaded by revolutionary troops, and in 1795 the Duchy was annexed to the French Republic under the name of the "Department of the Forests." The local institutions of the country were now suppressed, the Church was persecuted, the people were conscripted into the French armies; and, although under the First Empire some of the hardships of revolutionary rule were mitigated, the Luxemburgers rejoiced when 1815 brought about the departure of the French.

The fall of Napoleon and the Congress of Vienna resulted in the restoration of Luxemburg's national independence. Its native dynasty had, of course, disappeared long since, but the Duchy, now raised to the status of a Grand Duchy, was given to the head of the House of Orange-Nassau, William I, King of the Netherlands, in compensation for the loss of his possessions in Germany, which had been ceded to the King of Prussia. The new Grand Duchy, connected with the Netherlands only by a personal union, was also made a member of the Germanic Confederation which, created by the Congress of Vienna to fill the void caused by the dissolution of the Holy Roman Empire in 1806, survived until 1866. The city of Luxemburg, declared a Federal fortress, received a Prussian garrison. Luxemburg's first Grand Duke was a sincere and hard-working ruler, but the very qualities which made him loved in the northern part of his dominions, that is to say, the present Kingdom of the Netherlands, lost him the confidence of his Belgian provinces. In 1830 Belgium revolted against him, to obtain its independence in the following year, and Luxemburg was involved in the Belgian movement. The conflict between Belgium and Holland was in one respect unfortunate for the Grand Duchy, for in the final settlement, concluded in 1839, five of its eight districts, including all but the entire Walloon region, were detached and formed into the Belgian Province of Luxemburg. On the other hand, what remained of the Grand Duchy was placed under the guarantee of the European Powers and thus saw its international status consolidated and confirmed.

Under the next two Grand Dukes, William II and William III of the Netherlands and of Luxemburg, the Grand Duchy prospered although, after the Austro-Prussian War of 1866, its independence was threatened for a moment by Napoleon III, who made overtures to William III for its purchase. Bismarck, on learning of the offer, protested forcibly against the annexation to France of what he claimed to be a Germanic land, whereupon Napoleon retorted with a demand for the withdrawal of the Prussian garrison from Luxemburg, which, after the dissolution of the Germanic Confederation, had ceased to be a Federal fortress. In 1867 the Conference of the Great Powers met in London to regulate the status of the Grand Duchy, and declared it to be an independent state, perpetually neutral under the collective guarantee of the signatory Powers, namely, Great Britain, Austria, Belgium, France, Russia and Prussia. The Conference also decreed the evacuation of Luxemburg by the Prussian garrison and the dismantling of the fortress. On the 9th September, 1867, the last battalion of the Prussian garrison left Luxemburg, and for the first time for many centuries the guard was mounted by native troops. But for the

Treaty of London, Luxemburg would undoubtedly have ceased to exist as an independent country; and the fact that London should have been chosen as the venue for the Congress that was to perpetuate its independence is an interesting link in the chain of events connecting Luxemburg with England, the first of which was forged when an English Saint, Willibrord of Northumbria, converted the Luxemburgers to Christianity at the beginning of the eighth century.

William III, who had been represented in Luxemburg for the greater part of his reign by his popular brother Henry with the title of Prince-Lieutenant of the Grand Duke, died in 1890 without surviving male issue, and was succeeded in the Netherlands by his daughter, the present Queen Wilhelmina. Under the Salic Law, which applied to Luxemburg, females were excluded from the succession, and this now passed to the head of the senior branch (that of Walram) of the House of Nassau, which had separated from the branch of which the Dutch kings were the head (that of Otto) in the thirteenth century. Adolphus, the new Grand Duke, was already a man of seventy-three and had experienced some remarkable changes of fortune when he ascended his new throne. Born in 1817, he had succeeded his father as reigning Duke of Nassau as far back as 1839, and ruled there until 1866, when, having espoused the unsuccessful cause of Austria in the Austro-Prussian War, he, together with the King of Hanover and Austria's other German allies, had to suffer the annexation of their territories by Prussia and to go into exile. For the next quarter of a century he led the existence of a *prince en exil,* little foreseeing, it may well be supposed, that he would survive to reign over another country for a farther period of fifteen years. Adolphus of Nassau is probably the only monarch in history who struck coins in one country with a German legend, with a French legend in another. He died in 1905 at the age of eighty-eight and, had his reign been uninterrupted, he would have been a ruling sovereign for sixty-six years.[1] His son and successor, the Grand Duke William IV, died in 1912, leaving six daughters but no son, and the Nassau Family Pact, to which the Salic Law is subordinate, now came into play. The Pact provides that, in the event of the complete extinction of males, the rights of succession pass to the daughter or nearest heiress of

[1] The longest reigns of recent European history have been :

	Reigned
Charles Frederick, Margrave (later Grand Duke) of Baden	1738–1811
Louis XIV of France	1643–1715
John II of Liechtenstein	1858–1929
Francis Joseph I of Austria	1848–1916
Ferdinand IV of Naples (III of Sicily, I of the Two Sicilies)	1759–1825
Frederick Augustus I, Elector (later King) of Saxony	1763–1827
Queen Victoria	1837–1901
Charles III of Lorraine	1545–1608
Honoré III of Monaco	1733–1795*
Christian IV of Denmark	1588–1649
Nicholas I, Prince (later King) of Montenegro .	1860–1921†
King George III	1760–1820

* No longer *de facto* after 1793.
† No longer *de facto* after 1918.

the last male; and in accordance with this provision William's eldest daughter, Mary Adelaide, became Grand Duchess. There was thus created the anomalous situation that Queen Wilhelmina, unable to succeed in Luxemburg on account of her sex, now found a woman on the throne that she had lost. Similar would have been the situation in which Queen Victoria would have found herself had King Ernest Augustus of Hanover been succeeded by a woman.

The story of Mary Adelaide's reign of seven years is truly a tragic one. The first sovereign of Luxemburg to be born on Luxemburg's soil, her accession to the throne at the age of eighteen was greeted with the utmost enthusiasm throughout her little country. But barely two years later came the outbreak of the Great War and Germany's cynical occupation of the helpless Grand Duchy. Too small and powerless to oppose the German invasion by force of arms as Belgium had done, the Grand Duchess and her people were confined to the passive rôle of protesting against this flagrant breach of international agreements and of awaiting with such patience as they could muster the day that the fortunes of war would free their country. When that day came, more than four years later, the Grand Duchess was in the painful position common to many who have to steer a neutral course between two conflicting elements. While Berlin denounced as "hostile to Germany Mary Adelaide's pro-Luxemburg policy," there were those among the Allies who regarded her with suspicion as having displayed pro-German sentiments during the occupation. Moreover, there developed a strong tendency in Belgium to press for the annexation of the Grand Duchy, and of this tendency certain subversive elements in the Grand Duchy itself, born of Bolshevism and the sufferings of the War, took advantage to attempt to depose the dynasty. A *démarche* made by the Luxemburg Government in December, 1918, with the object of entering into negotiations with the French Government, met with the reply of the French Foreign Minister that "he was unable to receive the Ministers of the Grand Duchess of Luxemburg." And so in January, 1919, the poor young Grand Duchess, alone and friendless and menaced on every side, abdicated and entered a convent, dying in 1924 as a Carmelite nun. Sad was the lot that fell to Sœur Marie des Pauvres, as Mary Adelaide became after her abdication, and not only sad but undeserved, as may be judged from the monument that rises conspicuously in the upper part of the city of Luxemburg to the Luxemburgers who fought and died with the Allies. Her sister Charlotte, who succeeded her, decided to make the wishes of the people clear to the world once and for all by means of a referendum; and the result of the plébiscite held in September, 1919, was decisive. 80 per cent. of the voters pronounced in favour of the Grand Duchess Charlotte, 19 per cent. for a Republic; and the Grand Duchess could say thereafter without fear of contradiction that she was the legitimate sovereign of the land not only by hereditary right but by the will of the people freely expressed. Five weeks after the holding of the plébiscite the Grand Duchess married Prince Felix of Bourbon Parma, and in 1921 was born her eldest son, who was christened John after Luxemburg's hero, the King of Bohemia. One may hope that Luxemburg's second Grand Duchess will have a happier and more peaceful reign than her unfortunate predecessor.

In the literal sense of the words the existence of Luxemburg's ruler can scarcely be a quiet one when he or she resides in the capital, for surely no other Royal residence can lack privacy to the same extent as the Grand Ducal Palace. A relic of the days of the Spanish occupation and picturesque enough so far as its sixteenth-century portions are concerned, it stands on the street without any garden; tramways pass within a few yards of it; it is adjoined on one side by houses that form a part of the same block, on the other side by the Chamber of Deputies. On the opposite side of the Palace is a cinema, while immediately in front of the façade is the establishment of a coffin-maker, whose wares are displayed in his front window. It is true that he does not, like so many shopkeepers of the capital, display the quartered arms, surmounted by the closed crown, of a *"fournisseur de la Couronne";* nevertheless a *memento mori* of this sort is not, one would think, the perfect *vis-à-vis.*

Luxemburg is one of the most picturesquely situated towns in Europe and has grown enormously since its

PLATE IV

The Grand Duchess Charlotte and Her Consort.

The Grand Ducal Palace, Luxemburg.

To face p. 116.

fortifications were dismantled, new quarters rising on the levelled walls and bastions of Vauban's defences. Fortunately, enough of the mediæval walls and towers has remained to preserve to the place its character of an ancient little *Residenz-stadt*. For a town of barely 60,000 inhabitants Luxemburg possesses what seems to be an astonishing number of hotels, but it must be remembered that many visitors wander in the summer through this land of roses.

The spoken language of the country is the Luxemburger dialect, which is a Middle High German speech with an admixture of Celtic and Latin words. It is the language not only of the entire Grand Duchy, with the exception of two Walloon-speaking villages, but also of the adjoining portions of Lorraine and Belgium and, oddly enough, of the "Saxons" of Transylvania at the other end of Europe. Both French and German are official languages, but French is the language habitually spoken in Parliament and is the language of pleadings in the Courts, likewise of the Grand Duchy's postage stamps and coins. Accused persons and witnesses give their evidence in German, while legislative and administrative Acts are printed in both languages. Most people in Luxemburg are bilingual; and the dynasty exemplifies in itself this blend of the Latin and the Teutonic. The Grand Duchy is wholly Catholic and remarkably devout, the churches being thronged, as in Malta, as much with men as with women.

With important mineral, horticultural and agricultural resources, with a smiling and attractive countryside, with a popular dynasty and a happy people, there should be a prosperous future in store for this largest of the minor states of Europe, now that its international position and internal institutions have survived in safety the turmoils and shocks of the Great War.

MYSTERY AND HISTORY IN FRANCONIA

V

MYSTERY AND HISTORY IN FRANCONIA

THE time is night of the 15th October, 1812; the scene, a bedroom in the Palace of Karlsruhe, the capital of the Grand Duchy of Baden. The baby son of the Grand Ducal pair, born in the previous month, is dead, and his mother is too ill to be allowed to see him before he is taken away. The child had a sister but no brothers, and the way to the throne is now open to the Grand Duke's wicked uncle, Louis, and, after him, to the children of his grandfather, Charles Frederick, by a morganatic wife, the Countess Hochberg. There is a ghost in the Royal family, the "White Lady" who walks before the deaths of princes of the Grand Ducal House, and the White Lady has been about this night on her mournful errand. But was it indeed the White Lady who was seen to glide noiselessly along the dim corridors of the Palace, or was it a living form, impersonating her for some evil purpose? That is the question which for many years agitated the good people of Baden and has never received a final answer. According to a conviction held passionately a century ago by many and not yet wholly abandoned, a minion of the wicked uncle played the part of the ghost while another minion seized the Royal infant, who was really alive, and substituted a dead babe in his place. Before the Grand Duchess had recovered (she was Stéphanie Beauharnais, the Empress Josephine's daughter by her first husband and the adopted daughter of Napoleon), the little body was buried; and six years later the child's father, the Grand Duke Charles, died without other male issue and the sinister uncle Louis became Grand Duke.

The scene now shifts to Franconia, where, a few miles to the south-east of Nuremberg and equidistant from those centres of two different arts, Oberammergau and Bayreuth, the placid little town of Ansbach recalls by means of its stately Louis XV château, with its charming park reminiscent of Fontainebleau and its pleasantly formal orangery, that it was once the *Residenz-stadt* of the Margraves of that place. In the park, known as the *Hofgarten*, stands the bust of a forgotten eighteenth-century poet, John Peter Uz, who is described thereon as "the lover of his kind" but is more suggestive, in name at all events, of the character in Genesis who is generally coupled with his brother Buz. And near the memorial to the lover of his kind there rises an octagonal column recording that on that spot was mortally wounded in 1833 the "mystery-child of Europe," Kaspar Hauser. *Hic occultus occulto occisus est* are the words inscribed upon one of its panels.

What is the connexion between the dead babe in the Palace of Karlsruhe and the young peasant who was stabbed twenty-one years later in the *Hofgarten* of Ansbach?

On Whit Monday of the year 1828 a worthy citizen of Nuremberg, loitering at the door of his house by the New Gate, was arrested by the sight of a lad in peasant's dress, apparently about sixteen or seventeen years of age, who seemed to be trying to walk into the town but was moving with unsteady gait and hesitating step as if unable to govern fully the movements of his legs. When accosted by the good burgher the lad said, speaking in the Bavarian dialect: "I want to be a trooper as my father was," and held out a letter addressed to the Captain of the fourth squadron of the Sixth Regiment of Bavarian Light Horse.

The Captain was out and the youth, who seemed to be half-witted, was taken to the stable and given some straw, on which he lay down and went soundly to sleep. When the Captain came home, he was awakened with difficulty and seemed unable to give an account of himself. The letter was not much more helpful. It was written in German, anonymously, and stated that the writer was a poor labourer, the father of ten children; that the youth had been left at his house when a baby in October, 1812, together with a memorandum in Latin, which was enclosed with the letter; and that the writer of the letter had been asked by the mother of the child, who was unknown to him, to bring the foundling up secretly and to give him instruction in reading, writing and Christianity. The Latin memorandum was to the following effect: "The child is already baptized; you must give him a surname yourself; you must educate him. His father was in the Light Horse. When he is seventeen years old send him to Nuremberg to the Sixth Regiment of Light Horse, for there his father was. He was born on the 30th April, 1812. I am a poor girl and cannot support him. His father is dead."

The Captain determined to have nothing to do with the matter and handed the lad over to the police, who proceeded to make a close examination of the mysterious arrival. The only sign of identification upon him was a white handkerchief marked "K. H." He was of medium height, broad of shoulder and well built; his skin was fine and white and his hands were small and beautifully formed. But he bore two physical peculiarities: his knee-joints, instead of projecting when the leg was straightened, formed a depression, while the soles of his feet were quite soft and were covered with blisters. While being examined he continued to point to his feet with cries of pain. One of the officials, taking compassion on him, offered him some meat and beer. He rejected these with signs of aversion but eagerly partook of bread and water. Beyond his constantly reiterated statement: "I want to be a trooper as my father was," nothing could be got out of him; but, when writing materials were produced, he took a pen and wrote slowly the words "Kaspar Hauser." The officials, unable to decide whether the youth was a half-wit or was playing a part, removed him to a tower near the Guard House where vagrants and such like persons were wont to be confined. Here he was treated kindly and gradually learned to speak, or at all events began to indulge in the practice of speaking, and to converse with those around him. By degrees, as he became more and more communicative, he gave the following account of himself:—He did not know who he was or whence he came, nor could he remember ever having lived elsewhere than in a subterranean hole in a state of semi-darkness, always sitting on the ground with his back supported in an erect position, a statement which appeared to be corroborated by the condition of his knees. He had been fed only on bread and water, which were brought to him daily by a man whose face he had never seen. This man taught him to write the letters composing the name Kaspar Hauser. One night the man took him on his shoulders and deposited him by the gate of Nuremberg, where he was found by the citizen. And this was all that he could be induced to say.

Kaspar's condition and behaviour seemed to be consistent with this extraordinary tale. For some time it was evident that he could not walk without stumbling. It caused, or appeared to cause him great pain to attempt to put on boots. He seemed to be unable to control his limbs, and his eyes became inflamed in the daylight. When he first saw the flame of a candle he was so delighted that he put his finger into it. Altogether, he displayed such ignorance of physical things and of the world around him that those observing him found

it difficult to believe that he was a fraud. Soon, while
the lad was becoming by degrees more accustomed to
his new surroundings, the story of his discovery began
to spread not only through Germany but abroad, and
from many countries not only the curious, but serious
investigators, flocked to Nuremberg to behold this phenomenon, loading him with presents, which generally
took the form of toys. By July, 1828, the city of Nuremberg, to which Kaspar was proving a valuable attrac-
tion, had adopted him and had sent him to live with a
schoolmaster named Daumer, who was to undertake
his education; and Kaspar proved so apt a pupil that
within a year he had composed and written a work of
autobiography. His tutor, and a jurist named Paul
Anselm von Feuerbach, President of the Court of
Appeal in Ansbach, now studied him carefully and came
to the conclusion that he was a "sensitive" and a remarkable example of that "animal magnetism" which
was being much discussed in Germany at that time.
Meanwhile, the minute examination to which his story
was being subjected began to breed suspicions, soon
swelled by rumour into a widespread belief, that here
was no peasant; for was a poor woman anxious to get
her child adopted likely to deposit it at the door of a
labourer with ten children of his own, or to expect him
to support it for seventeen years? It was felt that the
mysterious "sensitive" must be of noble if not of Royal
birth. Some averred that he was a son of Napoleon, but
the popular belief soon inclined to the theory that he

was the only son of the Grand Duke Charles of Baden, who had been spirited away alive in the manner suggested at the beginning of this chapter, while a dead child had been buried in his place. According to this belief the child had been confined in a dark hovel so that, if he grew up at all, it would only be as an imbecile unable to learn or betray the secret of his origin; and the holders of this theory were strengthened in their conviction when an attempt was made to put Kaspar out of the way just when his mind was approximating to that of a normal being of his age. On the 17th October, 1829, he felt unwell and was excused from attending his mathematical class, and was allowed to stay at home at Herr Daumer's house. Shortly after noon, a servant, while sweeping, noticed spots of blood and bloody footmarks on the floor and, following them to the cellar, found Kaspar lying there unconscious with a wound across his forehead, apparently made with a razor. For some time he was in a state of delirium, during which he kept on murmuring: "Man come—do not kill me— I love all men—have done no one anything—man, I love you too—do not kill—why man kill?" When the lad had sufficiently recovered, a judicial inquiry was held but revealed nothing. Kaspar himself said that a masked man entered the house and felled him to the ground; he could only explain how he got into the cellar by the theory that he had crawled there in a semiconscious condition. Feuerbach thought that the murderer had attempted to cut Kaspar's throat and that the

127

lad, by ducking, had received the blow on his forehead.

Among the prominent people whose attention was
drawn to the case by this episode was the fourth Earl
Stanhope, the grandfather of the late Lord Rosebery.
In May, 1831, Lord Stanhope came to Nuremberg and
became so interested in the lad that he made financial
provision for him and removed him from Nuremberg
to place him in the charge of a certain Dr. Meyer in
Ansbach. It was here that Kaspar came under the direct
observation of Feuerbach, who had been studying his
case since 1828 and now gave him a small appointment
as clerk to the Registrar of his Court. So well did he
acquit himself here that Lord Stanhope now thought of
adopting him and of taking him to England; and it was
this circumstance which, according to the adherents of
the Baden theory, led to the tragedy that followed. At
this point it should be mentioned that the wicked Grand
Duke Louis, the last male of the non-morganatic line of
the House of Zähringen, had died in 1830 and had been
succeeded, under a Pragmatic Sanction specially en-
acted, by his father's morganatic son by the Countess
Hochberg. On the evening of the 14th December, 1833,
as Kaspar was returning home from his work, a man in
a blouse brought him a message from a Palace gardener
that he should come at once to the *Hofgarten*. He went
there—this is his own deposition, made before he lost
consciousness and died—and, when he reached the
monument of the poet Uz, a man came forward, gave

him a bag, stabbed him and ran away. Kaspar was found to have a narrow wound under the centre of the left breast, which was evidently caused by a dagger and had penetrated the heart.

The police made every effort to discover the murderer, but without success, nor was the weapon ever found. The King of Bavaria, who was an interested party in that he was a claimant to the Grand Duchy of Baden if the dynasty of Zähringen should become extinct, caused an inquiry to be made into the case, while Feuerbach and Daumer now publicly sponsored the theory that the murdered lad was the Crown Prince of Baden. The motive of the murder, according to this theory, was that those interested in Kaspar's suppression decided to put him out of the way before Lord Stanhope could remove him in safety to England. Feuerbach wrote that: "there are circles of human society into which the arm of justice dares not penetrate," and the affair aroused a great sensation and produced a prolonged literary controversy. Lord Stanhope ultimately inclined to the belief that Kaspar had killed himself, possibly without intending to do so (for snow was lying where Kaspar was stabbed, but only one set of footprints was found); and in the end, by the irony of fate, he was himself accused of having contrived his protégé's death. As late as 1893 the Duchess of Cleveland, Lord Stanhope's daughter and Lord Rosebery's mother, found it necessary to reply to this accusation. But the evidence of the story of Kaspar Hauser's life and death is hopelessly involved and the whole truth will probably never be known. He was buried in the churchyard of S. John's Church (beneath which is the vault of the Margraves), while there is actually a special museum in Ansbach, the Kaspar Hauser Museum, to display the relics of the mystery-child of Europe.

Before we pass from Kaspar Hauser, it may be recalled that Lord Stanhope is not Ansbach's only connexion with England. One of the most capable of the English Queens-Consort was a Princess of Ansbach: Caroline, daughter of the Margrave John Frederick and wife of George II. On four occasions Queen Caroline was Regent during her husband's absences from England, and her influence in English politics, strongly exercised in support of Walpole, was as considerable as it was salutary. Her grandson, George III, made much use in the American War of Independence of Ansbach mercenaries, hired to him by their Margrave despite the indignation of his uncle, Frederick the Great. And it was owing to his devotion to an Englishwoman, Elizabeth, Lady Craven, whom he married in 1791, when he was a widower and she a widow, that the last of the Margraves, Christian Frederick, sold his dominions to Prussia in order to end his days with her at Brandenburgh House in London. It is not often that territories which have fallen into Prussia's greedy maw have been able to extricate themselves from that allegiance; Prussia is not unlike that

"Bight of Benin,
Whence few come out though many go in."

130

To Ansbach has befallen this rare experience, for in 1806 Napoleon took it away from Prussia to add it to Bavaria, and Bavarian it has remained.

So much for this early nineteenth-century mystery, imposed upon the French eighteenth-century *décor* of the Palace of the Margraves. But there is another side to Ansbach, that South German mediæval side which Franconia displays so pre-eminently well. Ansbach is by no means only a little Versailles transplanted into a corner of Bavaria; in addition to its placid baroque it contains a gem of the art and spirit of the Middle Ages. The nucleus of Ansbach town is the monastic Church of S. Gumbert, a Benedictine foundation dating from the twelfth century. Much of the original fabric of this church has been rebuilt in heavy fashion in later times, but the fifteenth-century choir survives as one of the most perfect examples of Teutonic Gothic, a lofty, airy, graceful shrine of delicate traceries, fine vaulting and narrow lancet windows. This choir was the chapel of the Knights of the Swan, an Order founded in 1460 by the delightfully named Margrave Albert Achilles, who sought to raise the moral standard of the knight-hood of the time and chose the swan as the symbol of purity and goodness. Here in a semicircle stand the life-sized stone effigies of Albert Achilles's paladins, sur-mounted by their banners and coats-of-arms, making of their chapel the embodiment of mediæval chivalry and heraldry and romance.

Should the visitor to Ansbach feel tempted to pro-

131

long his impressions among the Knights of the Swan by continuing to immerse himself for a few days in the quintessence of German mediævalism, then let him seek, but a few miles away, that western corner of Bavaria where the Swabian Jura and the Franconian Highlands meet and the towns of Rothenburg, Dinkelsbühl and Nördlingen, each formerly a Free City of the Holy Roman Empire, carry into the twentieth century the body and spirit of the fourteenth and the fifteenth. Rothenburg—"Rothenburg above the Tauber," to give it the full name which distinguishes it from the nineteen other German Rothenburgs—is probably the best known to the world at large of this delicious trio, being what is known as "an artist's paradise." Every other house in the town seems to contain a shop for the sale of etchings and photographs of its streets and monuments; but, if it is something of a professional beauty in this respect, its loveliness is for that very reason unquestionable. Whether it be its unbroken circle of walls, gates and bastions, within which the little city dominates the valley of the Tauber, whether it be its noble town-halls—the Gothic and the Renaissance— that rise side by side in its midst, the "Herren-strasse" with the houses of its old patrician families, its Gothic Church of S. James whose lofty, narrow proportions suggest Beauvais, or whether it be the general aspect of its streets, full of variety in detail but of a rare uniformity in purity of style, everything is as perfect of its kind as one can expect to find in this imperfect world.

PLATE V

One of the Gates of Dinkelsbühl.

Ansbach : The Kaspar
Hauser Monument.

The Town-Halls of Rothenburg.

[To face p. 132.

As one surveys the town from the top of the Rathaus tower, looks down upon its winding lanes, its high-pitched, red-tiled gables, its gates and walls and fortifications, one looks down upon a South German San Gimignano delle Belle Torri, not only because of its many towers but because here, too, one is surveying a town whose mediæval character and features have survived the centuries complete and unimpaired.

If Rothenburg suggests San Gimignano, Dinkels-bühl suggests the scenery of "Faust," but with the artificiality of the stage converted into reality. The monumental Church of S. George, late Gothic with a Romanesque porch, the cobbled streets of exceptional breadth, the dear little gabled houses all happily out of alignment, the varied colours of their façades (red, yellow and a delightful green—something between apple and emerald—which must, I think, be peculiar to Dinkelsbühl), the inns with their cheerful projecting signs, its perfect walls and *chemin-de-rond*, its real moat with real water and real swans, all these things create an *ensemble* of picturesqueness that it would be difficult to match. Dinkelsbühl is not a whit less complete, less unspoiled than Rothenburg, but it is smaller, more *intime;* and whoever sees it in winter-time, with the snow on its roofs and its burghers skating on the moat, with the market-place devoted to the sale of young pine trees and other seasonable commodities, will find it, I am sure, the very embodiment of the spirit of Christmas.

Nördlingen makes an impression of another sort; it is less gay, less smiling. This is partly due to the fact that the timbering of the houses, so delightful a feature of Rothenburg and Dinkelsbühl, is here generally concealed, partly to the heavier, more massive character of its walls and towers. These do not, as in the case of Rothenburg, greet the visitor from afar nor, as in Dinkelsbühl, rise gracefully above the surrounding water; they sit solidly in the hollow, as if conscious that neither the Thirty Years' War nor any other commotion could disturb them. Nördlingen's great Church of S. George, too, is colder than its namesake of Dinkelsbühl, probably because it has passed, unlike the other, into the ownership of the Reformed Church. Was it not Heine who said of Lutheran churches that they are decorated only with gigantic movable Psalm numbers? In other ways, however, it still respects pre-Reformation tradition: nightly from the top of its great tower, which for some unexplained reason the citizens call "Daniel," is heard the call of the night-watchman. I noticed another example of respect for tradition, interesting in a different way. Before the Holy Roman Empire, with its 173 secular and ecclesiastical monarchies and its 51 Free Cities, died of old age, Nördlingen was surrounded by the territory of the Princes of Oettingen; and some of the shops still display the Oettingen arms as purveyors to their present Serene Highnesses, although the family has been mediatized since the beginning of the nineteenth century.

The three towns lie on the old military road through Franconia and Swabia and have passed through tempestuous times, especially in the Thirty Years' War, which raged with particular violence in this part of Germany. It is from incidents in this troubled period of their history that the historical plays—given by the people of each of the towns on Sundays in summer—are drawn. The episode commemorated in Rothenburg's play, the "Meistertrunk," is perhaps the most original. The year is 1631. Rothenburg is in alliance with the Swedes, who have a detachment in the town; outside the walls, in great force, lies Tilly, the Imperial Generalissimo. Tilly demands and expects surrender; the citizens determine to make a stand. But their resistance is brief and Tilly is soon inside the walls and in occupation of the Rathaus, where, angered at the unnecessary bloodshed, he announces that the lives of four of the town-councillors shall be taken to punish the Council for their futile opposition. They seek to placate him, and the cellarer's daughter offers him wine in the ceremonial glass beaker reserved for the visits of the Emperor. Tilly, who is not a wine-drinker, tastes and likes the wine and wonders at the mighty goblet, which holds no fewer than thirteen pints. A thought occurs to him: he will spare the councillors if one of them can empty it at a draught. The ex-burgomaster, Nusch, volunteers and is successful, and saves himself and his colleagues by his heroic capacity.

Dinkelsbühl, predominantly Catholic, was on the

Imperial side. But in 1632, the period of its play, the Imperial troops had been forced to withdraw and the Swedish Colonel Sperreut was on the point of entering the defenceless town. Helplessly the citizens await the sack of their little city at the hands of the Swede when the maiden Lore, the daughter of the keeper of one of the towers, hoping to find a way to soften his heart, leads the schoolchildren to his camp to implore mercy. A little boy reminds Sperreut of a recently lost son, he relents, and the town is spared.

Dinkelsbühl's "Kinderzeche" is essentially a children's festival; in Nördlingen's play a love-interest is the central feature. Here the loyalties are different. Nördlingen, strongly Protestant, defies the Emperor with the help of the Swedes, while a romance develops between the Swedish Commander and the burgomaster's beautiful daughter. The play is written round the first of the two battles of Nördlingen, fought in 1634, when the hitherto unbeaten Swedish army was defeated with great loss by the Imperialists and the Spaniards; and, together with the plays of Dinkelsbühl and Rothenburg, creates an additional inducement to visit these well-preserved relics of the Middle Ages.

HISTORY AND
MYSTERY-PLAY
IN SALZBURG

HISTORY AND MYSTERY-PLAY IN SALZBURG

THERE are still left in Europe one or two towns that recall to mind the lines:

> "The Prince-Bishop muttered a curse, and a prayer,
> Which his double capacity hit to a nicety:
> His Princely, or Lay, half induced him to swear,
> His Episcopal moiety said '*Benedicite.*' "

Trent, whose princely-episcopal castle cannot have been unknown to the author of the *Ingoldsby Legends*, is one of these; and another, emphatically, is Salzburg. If in Trent there seem to have prevailed, notwithstanding its conciliar associations, the lay qualities of its ruling *porporati*, in Salzburg, at the first glance, it is otherwise. Salzburg looks what she is, a small university town with a strong ecclesiastical impress. Her public buildings—and they appear to outnumber the others—display prominently in pink or brown marble the arms of their several archiepiscopal founders; her churches are numerous enough for a town three times her size; while the Kapuzinerberg with its Friary overlooking the right bank of the Salzach, the Nonnberg with the Gothic convent of Benedictine nuns overlooking the left, seem emblematic of the town over which they watch. Yet one needs not to be in Salzburg for long to understand that the arms which bore the crozier could be equally effective with the sword; that the acropolis of Salzburg, the formidable Hohensalzburg, which dwarfs both Nonnberg and Kapuzinerberg, dominates the town and the entire countryside in a manner that is not so much pastoral as minatory. Typical feudal mediæval fortress, this grim stronghold suggests, despite its superlative picturesqueness, anything but the word *Benedicite*. Here, in 1525, Archbishop Matthew Lang withstood behind its turrets and battlements a siege of citizens and peasants endeavouring to break the power of the Prince-Archbishops and to make Salzburg a free city; here, early in the next century, the curiously named Archbishop Marcus Sitticus imprisoned his predecessor Wolf Dietrich, one of Salzburg's great builders, for the five years preceding the latter's death; here the prevailing sound was not the *Angelus* but the roar of that monstrous contrivance that summoned the prelate's lieges to his standard; here a well-appointed torture chamber, still to be visited, accommodated those who questioned the political rather than the spiritual authority of Salzburg's lords. Perhaps it was on this account that the rule of the Prince-Archbishops was so enduring, surviving even the explosive effects of the French Revolution. Although secularized in 1802, it was not until after Waterloo that the Duchy of Salzburg was incorporated with the

Austrian Empire; a tablet outside the Mirabell-Schloss recounts how the grounds of that lovely little palace were made over to the citizens of Salzburg in 1866 by the Emperor Francis Joseph to celebrate the fiftieth anniversary of the transfer.

For all that they were Prince-Primates of Germany and *Legati Nati* of the Holy Roman Church (the holders of the see retain these titles to the present day), Salzburg's sovereign archbishops were not able entirely to resist the advance of the Reformed religion into their dominions, nor were their lives in all cases precisely edifying according to modern ecclesiastical standards. Their wealth was enormous—the extensive salt mines of the whole Salzkammergut were their exclusive appanage—but, although they could coerce the peasants into remaining within the fold of the Roman obedience, they had not the same hold over the salt-miners, skilled and specialized workmen on whom they were dependent for their revenues from the mines. Among the miners, keen-minded and progressive, the new teaching had made more headway than among the less speculative, more docile peasant-farmers, with the anomalous result that the strongest and most enduring reformed communities in the Catholic portions of the Holy Roman Empire were those established in the ultra-Catholic domains of the Prince-Archbishops of Salzburg. If the visitor to the Salzkammergut to-day is surprised to see in such essentially Catholic villages as Hallstadt, Aussee, Gosau and others a Reformed parish

141

church side by side with the Roman, it is to the indis-
pensability of the salt-miners to the Prince-Archbishops
that he must attribute this unexpected juxtaposition.

Owing allegiance only to the Pope and the Holy
Roman Emperor and, as we have seen, extremely rich,
the Archbishops not infrequently allowed, it is to be
feared, their princely or lay to prevail over their episcopal moiety in their private lives. The fact that
Salzburg is so full of palaces is due partly, no doubt,
to the wealth and passion for building of Salzburg's
Lords, but partly, too, to the necessity for suitably
housing the episcopal mistresses. They certainly look
anything but Fathers in God, these lordly prelates, in
the portraits that adorn their monuments in the transept
of their Cathedral. Rather do they suggest the Heavy
Dragoon of the Thirty Years' War in clerical fancy
dress as they crouch at their faldstools, clumsy, peruked
and truculent, in an ungainly and evidently unaccus-
tomed attitude of devotion. One almost fancies one
discerns the armour underneath the cassock. But if the
rulers of Salzburg were not always gentle and not always
virtuous, they were at all events intellectually enlight-
ened and generous patrons of art in all its forms. And
it is pleasant to find that, while so many Austrians are
doing their best to obliterate their history, even to the
extent of being willing to surrender their nationality
in favour of that of their north-western neighbours,
the Salzburgers have the good taste—possibly also the
worldly wisdom—to cherish the traditions fostered by

a long line of cultured if autocratic and tyrannous prelates. Friars and nuns wander about Gothic cloisters as
they did in the Middle Ages; the Court Pharmacy of
the Prince-Archbishops—*mutatis mutandis* the Lock of
Salzburg—still displays its physicks and cordials and
unguents behind its original shutters; you take your
tea or coffee at Tomaselli's precisely as did the contemporaries of Mozart. Government Departments and
offices are housed in the stately old palaces of the
archiepiscopal régime; and it is distinctly pleasant
to buy, in the Post Office under the Glockenspiel-
tower, a money-order in a room entered by a fine
old door of hand-wrought iron and decorated with the
heraldic achievements of the Most Serene and Reverend
Count Paris Lodron, a magnificent ruler of the seventeenth century. Some, even, of the traditions of more
recent times have survived the changes of 1918. The
Churfürst-strasse recalls the days when Salzburg's
princes were also members of the Electoral College;
Toskana-strasse, the fact that the last Grand Duke of
Tuscany found asylum here after he lost his throne in
1860. And in Salzburg's immediate vicinity still lives,
now that she has had to leave the *Residenz*, his widow,
become, by the death of the late Queen of the Two
Sicilies, the only surviving consort of a ruler of the
Italian States which disappeared with the unification of
Italy.

Salzburg's dominant architectural notes are Gothic
and baroque (the Austrian domestic baroque, it will be

generally admitted, exhibits the style in its most attractive manifestation); and the two principal forms of entertainment she has been offering to her visitors since the genius of Reinhardt converted an occasional and haphazard series of concerts into an annual event of the first musical and dramatic importance correspond in a sense with the two main types of her architecture. Her musical attractions—"Don Giovanni," "The Marriage of Figaro," orchestral and chamber-music concerts, organ-recitals in the Cathedral—"featuring," in the theatrical jargon of the day, the works of Mozart, her greatest son, and his contemporaries, recall, as do her rococo squares and streets, the gentle calm of the eighteenth century, with which a modern work such as Strauss's *Rosenkavalier* is equally in keeping. Her Gothic spirit lives as brightly in the morality plays, which have long been one of Salzburg's traditions. First in the Collegiate Church of S. Peter, then in front of the Cathedral, and now, also, in the riding-school of the Prince-Archbishops has been performed a notable series of mystery-plays, old and new, such as "The Miracle," Hoffmannsthal's *Jedermann* and his awkwardly named "Salzburg World Theatre" and Mell's "Apostle Play," to which in 1927 there was added the *Pärchenspiel* of Billinger, a mystical peasant drama. The riding-school, ingeniously adapted as a permanent theatre for the Salzburg festivals, answers the purpose admirably. The ecclesiastical atmosphere of the plays it houses is cleverly suggested, the open timber roof

144

might well be that of a fourteenth-century Italian basilica, the acoustics are excellent. And the adjoining summer riding-school, with boxes cut in tiers out of the solid rock, constitutes an admirable *pendant*, delightful for open-air orchestral concerts in fine weather.

Reinhardt's genius for stage-management is only equalled by his *flair* for discovering talent. Visitors to Salzburg in 1925, the first year that the riding-school was used for these performances, will long remember Lady Diana Cooper as the Madonna and Rosamund Pinchot as the erring nun; while Reinhardt's outstanding discovery of that year, next to Miss Pinchot, was Hans Moser, the comic relief in the "World Theatre." Not less memorable was the Jedermann of Moissi, who has set his seal on the part for all time. *Jedermann* as presented in the beautiful poetical version of Hugo von Hoffmannsthal differs from the old English *Everyman* in that the Tudor play leaves Everyman's former life to the imagination, while the other shows us, in riotous episode, the existence he led before death called him to a repentant and edifying end. From the æsthetic and the dramatic points of view this is all to the advantage of the Salzburg play—a traditional people's play, be it remembered, to which Hoffmannsthal has but given a noble and infinitely moving poetical form.

On the steps of the golden baroque façade of the Cathedral—the first church in the Italian style to be erected on Germanic soil—a platform of plain wooden boards does service as the stage: facing it, in the square whose other sides are bounded by a wing of the *Residenz* and the Canons' apartments, rise in tiers the equally plain benches for the audience. As a Prologue there is heard from inside the Cathedral the voice of the Lord, summoning Death to call Everyman to judgment, while a singularly effective *obbligato* is played on the Cathedral organ. The play begins with sidelights on Everyman's daily life: his infatuation with his gold, his selfish although not deliberately ill-natured attitude towards the poor neighbour and the debtor and his pious old mother, his discussions with his boon companion regarding his plans for his amusement. Then comes the rollicking banqueting scene presided over by his mistress, interrupted by the grim summons which is heard by Everyman but not by his guests. Nothing could be more eerily dramatic than this awful call, now booming, now moaning as it comes from all parts of the town, from the roofs of the *Residenz*, from the top of the narrow Gothic tower of the Church of the Franciscans behind the audience, even, as it seems, from the loftily remote Hohensalzburg itself. His companions laugh at him and persuade him that the voices are an hallucination; he takes heart again and raises his glass, only to push it aside in terror at the sudden clang of bells. Is it a coincidence or is it a brilliant little effect on the part of the producer that Everyman, horror-struck, utters the words: "What bells are these?" at the very moment when the Cathedral belfry and the neighbouring Glockenspiel sound the hour of six?

PLATE VI

SALZBURG

At the foot of the Hohensalzburg.

" *Jedermann* " on the steps of the Cathedral.

The Summer Riding School.

[*To face p.* 146.

Finally, Everyman understands only too clearly that the summons is real and that he must obey it. Chastened and frightened, he begs his companions and his two cousins, the fat and the lean, to accompany him on the dread journey, but with one accord they make excuses and he is left to his fate alone. Yet not quite alone, because at this moment a figure, thin and shrouded, wriggles feebly on to the stage, Everyman's Good Deeds. To her there presently comes another female figure, that of Faith, and the two convince him that in a repentant death he may yet hope for pardon and redemption. When the coarse, hearty, bouncing, robust, argumentative, furry Devil comes leaping up to claim his prize, only to find him snatched away from under his very nose by these two tenuous, unearthly females, it is difficult not to feel that Everyman has been undeservedly lucky and the Devil not quite fairly dealt by.

Reinhardt's genius as a producer is as manifest in the extreme of simplicity as in the extreme of sumptuousness. Here, in harmony with the religious character of the play, is a minimum of apparatus with a maximum of effect. There is no background other than the Cathedral front, no scenery, little if any make-up. The characters walk straight from the square on to the stage; their costumes, while correctly mediæval and excellent in design, are of the simplest possible materials.

So perfect is everything—the play itself, the venue, the incidental music, the manner in which the natural and architectural surroundings are harnessed to the production—that it almost seems as if the very pigeons have been trained to their parts when they wheel over the square in sudden alarm as a burst of angelic music from inside the Cathedral proclaims that Everyman has found salvation.

NEW STATES
AND OLD IN
DALMATIA

VII

NEW STATES AND OLD IN DALMATIA

I

Albania Revisited

"Albania," wrote Gibbon, "is a country of which less is known than the interior of America"; and unknown and unlike other countries it has remained. Although it is the latest, it is also the most patriarchal of Western kingdoms; in customs and, fortunately, in costume, it is at least four centuries behind the rest of Europe. It is a country in parts of which, until recently, no one below the social rank of a Bey was allowed to eat rice; a country where the commercial value of a cock is assessed by the length of his crow; where alone in the world the Roman Catholic clergy, from archbishop to the merest Franciscan novice, wear bristling moustaches (but no beards), as their martial, virile flock would not respect them if they were clean shaven; where the present King, when yet President of the Albanian Republic, had his effigy on the stamps and coins and worked fourteen hours a day; a country which in a decade has sampled four capitals. This last phenomenon is not due, however, to mere capricious-

151

ness on the part of the Albanians; it is susceptible of a perfectly reasonable explanation. The present generation of men has seen what has never been seen before in the same measure, namely, the coming to life (in some cases the resurrection) of a number of independent states, not by the processes of evolution but by a stroke of the pen. But while the majority of these new or revived states have had, as in Warsaw, Tiflis, Riga, Baku and even Erivan, an obvious capital, with Albania it has been otherwise. Here—no one town having overwhelming claims—the selection of the capital was dictated by the fluctuating circumstances of the moment; and it was not until several places had been tried and found wanting that the choice fell on the previously unknown Moslem village of Tirana. Albania's first independent administration—the Provisional Government of Ismail Kemal Bey—made its headquarters at Valona, as did the "International Commission of Control" which guided for a time the destinies of the infant State of Shqipni; the Governments of Essad Pasha Toptani, which preceded and succeeded that of William of Wied, were established at Durazzo, which was likewise the capital of that troubled, fleeting Mbret during his six uneasy months of reign. Scutari was the headquarters of the "ten-kilometre zone" once administered by an Allied military force; while at Korcha (Koritza) in the south there functioned in 1916–17 the "Autonomous Province" of the same name. The new (and, it may be hoped, the more settled) era in independent Albania's brief but restless life, which followed the end of the Great War, saw yet another change of capitals: the extremities and the sea-board alike were left in favour of a centrally situated locality half-way between the northern and southern frontiers, in the fertile lowlands which intervene between the coast and the eastern ranges.

It is not surprising that Valona (Aulōn, Avlona), its first experiment as a capital, did not remain Albania's final choice. It was Ismail Kemal's own country—he now rests in the graveyard of a ruinous little mosque in the village of Kanina that looks down upon the deep bay of Valona, in one of the humblest graves that any leading statesman can ever have occupied—but it had no qualifications other than the circumstance that Kemal drew his strength from this region. It is true that its predecessor, Apollonia, flourished as a colony of the Corinthians; that its harbour is spacious and served the Normans for their expeditions against Byzantium in the eleventh and twelfth centuries. But across the bay lies the little island of Sáseno; and Sáseno, commanding both entrances and strongly fortified, is one of three enclaves (the two others being the island of Lágosta and the town of Zara, of which more later) that Italy has secured as *points d'appui* on the Albanian and Yugoslav coasts. The town of Valona itself, one and a half miles inland, is a straggling village, malarial from the adjoining lagoons and of no importance of any sort; Durazzo is little better.

It is no exaggeration to say that Tirana, a Moslem village lying in a predominantly Moslem region, consists at the moment of a bazaar, four mosques (of the cheerful Bosnian type, gaily adorned on the outside with frescoes of flowers and fruit, including even the unorthodox grape), several barracks and countless Legations (that of Great Britain alone still remains at Durazzo). I calculate that Tirana must have about one Legation to every 1,000 inhabitants, a record which I imagine no other capital can emulate or even approach now that Tsetinje, the only possible competitor in this respect, has ceased to be the capital of an independent country. Accommodation and social amenities for the members of the diplomatic world are, as it may be imagined, for the moment somewhat limited; but there is a Sports Club, at which the ladies of the Turkish Legation are constantly to be seen playing tennis, and Albanians (an untravelled people so far as Western Europe is concerned) are brought into social contact with the members of the foreign colonies. Moreover, hotels of a modest kind have risen concomitantly with the Legations, one of them, indeed, so thoroughly up to date that I remember seeing the ground floor still only a framework, but the first (and only other) storey finished and functioning, quite like the American sky-scraper which completes its flats, not in ascending order, but in the order in which they are leased. But Tirana, mere village that it has been hitherto, is rapidly undergoing the process which I may perhaps be allowed to call Angorization. King Zog is nothing if not provident, and his determination is to look to the future rather than to the present and to make of Tirana an ideal modern capital so far as the resources of his State will allow. So new roads have been aligned, old shanties being pulled down to enable this to be done; avenues of trees have been planted; public gardens laid out; sites reserved for ultimate public buildings. Those of the moment are temporary expedients of an unpretentious kind; and nothing can be more unassuming than the Royal residence. Opposite is the more substantial building occupied by the Queen Mother and the King's sisters; between them a miniature public garden has made its début; to the side is one of Tirana's brightly painted little mosques, flanked by the equally attractive *türbé* of some Moslem worthy.

While reflecting on Moslem worthies I was struck by the resemblance of the Albanian Moslems (originally, like their Bosnian and Cretan co-religionists, Christians who embraced Islam from political expediency) to their Georgian fellow-mountaineers, on whom their religion likewise sits somewhat lightly. If Moslem Georgians can twit their Christian compatriots with having remained Christians on account of their fondness for pork and wine, so can the Christians of Tirana smile when, during Ramadan, Moslem restaurants conduct "business as usual"—but with drawn curtains. A lofty stone tower erected by some Turkish Pasha of the seventeenth or eighteenth century is the outstand-

ing architectural feature of the old, the recently built
Parliament House that of the new Tirana; while between
the two is the market-place, filled on Thursdays with
picturesque men and women and their equally picturesque wares, but also the scene at times of a less attractive spectacle. For it is here that malefactors condemned to death are hanged and their bodies gibbeted
on market days *pour décourager les autres*.

Mention of the market-place suggests the thought
of money, which in Albania has become a matter of
singular complexity. In consequence of the important
position held economically and commercially in Albania
by Austria before the War, and despite the introduction
of a new monetary system, popular reckoning knows
only the Austrian crown—not the depreciated paper
crown converted in Austria at the rate of 10,000 to the
Austrian schilling, but the pre-War silver crown—with
this difference, that it has now only the intrinsic value
of its silver and is worth 62½ to the £ instead of 24 as
before the War. I have learned since visiting Albania
a thing which I had long wanted to know, namely, what
has become of the pre-War silver of the Latin Union
and Central and Eastern Europe. It has all—such of it
as has not been melted down—found a refuge in
Albania, where, whether it be franc, lira, drachma, leu,
perper, dinar or lev, it figures with the Austrian coins
under the generic name of crown. Five, two, one and
half-crown or franc pieces, or their equivalent, here
rejoice the eye wearied of sordid paper and the almost

equally sordid base metal, while it is historically pleasant to jingle once more in one's pocket a silver portrait gallery ranging from old King Nicholas and Francis Joseph backward through King Alexander Obrenovič, Prince Milan IV, the Kings of Sardinia and the Two Sicilies, Pio Nono and the Emperor Ferdinand to Napoleon, King of Italy, and Bonaparte, First Consul. Albania is also full of an equally heterogeneous accumulation of gold coins, known, irrespective of their provenance, as Napoleons; while the new coinage, already referred to, is also on a gold basis with the Albanian gold franc as its unit. Side by side with the note issue of the National Bank of Albania—an institution under Italian control—came, when Zog was still President, the new coinage. In gold there are pieces of 100 and 20 francs, the former bearing, as does the five-franc piece in silver, the portrait of Ahmed Zogu. In silver there is also a two-franc piece, of which more anon. There are subsidiary coins in nickel and bronze bearing the designation of qintals and leks, twenty qintals equalling one lek and five leks equalling one franc gold. The lek takes its name from (and bears the image of) that well-known Albanian hero, Alexander the Great of Macedon, lek being the Shqipetar form of Alexander. But the twenty-franc and two-franc pieces have an interest other than the numismatic or the financial. The agreement between the Albanian Government and the National Bank of Albania contained no clause whereby the former had the right to approve the designs of the coins; the latter consequently held that it had *carte blanche* in the matter. So the twenty-franc piece descended upon an astonished Albania bearing, indeed, upon the obverse the head of Skanderbeg but upon the reverse, instead of Skanderbeg's double-headed eagle (Albania's national emblem), an unmistakable lion of S. Mark. Similarly the two-franc piece displays a patently Roman eagle, who has certainly never had more heads than one.

His features reproduced for his people on coins and on the stamps, upon the walls of every shop in the country, above the Speaker's seat in the Chamber of Deputies (where he figures in oils, wearing the two Albanian Orders of the Bessa and Skanderbeg), Ahmed Zogu [1] is a ruler whose initials are symbolical of his permeation of the affairs of his country. It is literally the case that everything in Albania from A to Z comes under his notice and is vitalized by his energy. As none can fail to realize who have seen in his aide-de-camp's office the printed time-table of his daily routine, he is the hardest-worked man in Albania. And he has accomplished what he has at an age which recalls the days of Pitt: except for the brief interregnum of Mgr. Fan (more properly Theophanes) Noli, he has been in power, either as Prime Minister, President or King, since the age of twenty-eight.

The Albanian Government has not had the advan-

---

[1] On assuming the Crown His Excellency Ahmed Beg Zogu became His Majesty King Zog, exchanging the definite form of his name, the Albanian for "bird," for the indefinite form of the word.

tage, as have the Austrian Succession States, of inheriting railways, roads, public buildings and the ordinary apparatus of a territorial "going concern." The Turks, although they employed during the centuries of their rule in Albania a long succession of Albanian administrators and soldiers, many of whom conferred distinction on the Empire they served, gave Albania little or nothing in return. Albania was until lately almost the ónly independent country in the world without railways (even little Montenegro had, before the War, its railway from Antivari to Virbazar), for it is only recently that a beginning has been made with the construction of a line from Tirana to its port of Durazzo to supplement the road which was once the Roman Via Ignatia. The biggest building in the country is the former Vali's Qonaq at Scutari, which now houses the Prefect of Albania's northernmost province, the military and gendarmerie administration and the Mayor. Roads are still few and bad, and the air service, which regularly connects Tirana with Scutari, Valona and Korcha, provides a much-needed complement to the necessarily agile Ford. In matters of transport Albania went with scarcely an intervening stage from mule-back to the air.

It is along a fairly bumpy road, therefore, that one travels in about five hours from Tirana to Scutari, but the almost unbroken lines of beautifully flowering Judas trees that fringe it make amends for the imperfections of its surface. Scutari is a large straggling town with an architectural impress that, despite its considerable Christian population, is definitely Turkish, lying picturesquely among orchards and kitchen gardens on the southern shore of the Lake of the same name. While the domes and minarets of its mosques and its whitewashed, deep-eaved houses give it the appearance of some Central Anatolian town, the costumes of the Christian section of its inhabitants—here Roman Catholics—are the most elaborate in all Albania. From the Turkish citadel of Venetian origin that tops a rocky eminence at the southern end of the town an amazingly good and extensive view is to be obtained: at your feet the rich plain intersected by the rivers Drin and Bojana, to the north the great Lake with Mount Taraboš in the foreground and in the background the forbidding black mountains of Montenegro, to the north-east the snow-topped Prokleta range inhabited by the Catholic warrior-tribes of the Dukagjini.

From the Scutari landing-stage, which Aubrey Herbert in *Ben Kendim* rightly termed an unostentatious one, I once embarked in a craft rather smaller than a small Thames launch, and in eight hours crossed to the Montenegrin township of Rjeka at the head of the fjord that forms the northern prolongation of the Lake of Scutari. It was a delicious journey, broken only at midday by a brief stop at Virbazar for a meal of carp boiled in oil in a primitive Montenegrin *khan*. The Lake is magnificently framed in mountains, and the islets at its northern end are thickly overgrown with

PLATE VII

The King's Office.   Tirana.   The Albanian Parliament.

Execution of an Albanian Rebel at Scutari.

View from Scutari.   [To face p. 160.

asphodel, generally an overrated weed whose name alone is beautiful but here not unpleasing against the eau-de-Nil tones of the water. From Rjeka a steep but tolerable road leads up to Tsetinje.

II

ICHABOD

With the disappearance of Montenegro as an independent monarchy there came to an end the most picturesque political institution of its day in the western world. Until 1851 the Black Mountain was a theocracy under an hereditary Vladika (Prince-Bishop) and ceased to be this only because Danilo II, the successor of the Vladika Peter II, refused to take holy orders as he intended to marry. The last Vladika's full title was "Metropolitan of Scanderia and the Sea-coast, Archbishop of Tsetinje, Exarch of the Holy Throne of Ipek, Vladika of Tserna Gora, Peter II Petrovič Njeguš"; and Montenegro's last sovereign, although no longer a Bishop, carried well into the twentieth century the essence of Balkan mediævalism at its best. Warrior, poet, lawgiver, paternal despot, King Nicholas seemed proof against the drab levelling processes of modern times, as befitted one who had lived the first ten years of his life under the régime of an hereditary Prince-Metropolitan; his little capital, Tsetinje, most unassuming of townlets though it be, was none the less the last capital of feudalism in Europe. Even after he had proclaimed himself King in 1910, on the occasion of his golden jubilee as a ruler, Nicholas declined to give up the good old-fashioned feudal title of Lord; his last coins, struck in 1914, still bear the superscription: "by the Grace of God King and Lord of Montenegro—*Kral i Gospodar Tserne Gore.*"

I have called Tsetinje an unassuming townlet; in truth it is hardly more than a village, distinguished from other villages by the Royal residences and the Legations scattered with an air of being oddly out of place among its low, white-washed houses. If Tirana can boast one Legation to every thousand inhabitants, this record was easily beaten by Tsetinje with a population of under 5,000. It can be well imagined how largely the Court and the *corps diplomatique* loomed in the life of the little town, how fundamentally, almost catastrophically, its very face is altered by their disappearance. The forlorn Royal Palaces, the closed and empty Legations, are as it were a dead hand laid upon it; as for the King and his family, whatever may have been their shortcomings, their going has robbed the place of the mainspring of its existence. With the exception of Erivan, it is in its present state the most pathetic capital I have seen.

The melancholy that now broods over Tsetinje is generated, I think, in the King's Palace, a modest yellow-washed two-storied building more villa than palace in dimensions and design. Its gate locked, its windows shuttered, its external aspect suggests complete emptiness within; actually, its condition is more depressing than mere emptiness could ever be. How so, it will be asked, since none of its contents have been removed by the present Government, since everything has been left as it was when the Royal Family took their compulsory departure from the country? But there can be a realism about these things more painful than spoliation. The portraits of members of the Petrovič dynasty and of foreign sovereigns now hang askew on the walls of the reception rooms, in places the wall-paper is coming off, downstairs I saw the King's diamond-hilted dress sword lying carelessly on the billiard-table, while the floor of the room was littered with pistols, yataghans and other weapons in complete disorder. More personal touches were the clothes still hanging in the cupboards, the gramophone records lying open on the music stool in the boudoir of the King's un-married daughters. Everything in and about the house speaks silently of the vanished dynasty; and it is by an act of taste that strikes the visitor as needlessly bad that the present Government has renamed the street in which it stands—full as it is of Petrovič traditions—"King Alexander Street." However cogent were the reasons in favour of the incorporation of Montenegro into the greater Yugoslav entity, the Petrovič family has not been, after all, without its glories, has not been without its claims on the gratitude not only of its own subjects but of all Southern Slavs. Even those Monte-negrins who had little sympathy with Nicholas's equivocations in the latter part of the Great War now remember regretfully his individual acquaintance with what must have been a large proportion of his people, his paternal interest in all their affairs. If they cherish no animosity against Alexander of Yugoslavia, their old King's grandson, the personal touch is gone; despite its consciousness of Yugoslav unity, Tsetinje cannot be unconscious of the contrast between the old dispensation and the new. It was a Royal capital; it is now the *chef-lieu* of an outlying and rather hungry province. It was once the head of the house; it has become a poor relation. It had been the nerve-centre of Balkan politics; in the place of the "Father-in-law of Europe" it has received a *sous-préfet*.

Not the Palace alone, but all Tsetinje and its environs recall the vanished dynasty: *si monumentum requiris, circumspice.* A few hundred yards away, built against the side of a hill, is the old convent, once the residence of the Vladikas and now that of the Metropolitans of Montenegro, who succeeded to the spiritual half of the Vladika's functions. It is a rough, crude structure in thorough keeping with the character of the country, erected near the site of the earlier convent destroyed by the Turks in 1714, but its curiously squat arcades, supported by capitals standing immediately on their bases without intervening shafts, are not without a picturesqueness of their own. The small cathedral contained within the convent enclosure is almost filled by enormous sarcophagi of the Vladika Peter I and other members of the family; one of the old round towers still standing above it was formerly festooned with the heads of Turks captured in the family's endless border raids; another hill is topped by the mortuary chapel of the first Vladika, Danilo I, the founder of the dynasty; while the remains of the greatest and last of the Vladikas, Peter II, lie on the summit of historic Lovčen, which rises massively between the plateau of Tsetinje and the coast.

The Vladika Peter I, who is buried in the metropolitan church, was a truly typical product of his land and of his house. His long reign of forty-nine years, from 1781 to 1830, was filled with campaigns against the Turks, yet he found the time to achieve renown as a poet, and his diplomatic skill saved Montenegro from the political storms that engulfed the neighbouring Ragusa and the infinitely more powerful Venice. His greatest victory, gained at Krusa in 1796, cost the Turks 30,000 lives, including that of their leader Kara Mahmud Pasha, whose head is recorded to have formed thereafter one of the ornaments of Peter's room. Despite his warlike instincts he enforced obedience to the law on his people, to whom, notwithstanding their wildness, he was an adored ruler and a personal friend. The first act of his nephew Peter II on his accession was to canonize his uncle *motu proprio* (an act whose summary procedure shocked the more leisurely canonists—and canonizers—of the sister-church of Russia); and there can have been few other saints, at all events few other nineteenth-century saints, who, besides having been on terms of intimacy with all their compatriots, have decorated their apartments with the skulls of their enemies slain in battle.

Peter II was even more distinguished a poet than his uncle and fully as heroic a figure. Wearing the beard and long hair prescribed by the Orthodox Church for her hierarchy and clergy, which accentuated his height of six feet eight inches, his majestic appearance "might well," wrote Sir Gardner Wilkinson, who visited him in 1844, "command the respect of a primitive and war-like race." "The merit," continues Wilkinson, "of excelling in military exercises is a great recommendation in their chief, and though in these days it may appear a singular accomplishment for a bishop to hit with a rifle a lemon thrown into the air by one of his attendants, this feat of the Vladika adds to the confidence he enjoys among his troops." It will, I think, be agreed that this is no unworthy personage to find his last resting-place on the summit of his country.

Alas that with the Royal Family there has disappeared from the Black Mountain, or has almost disappeared, the brilliant national dress, which was worn by none more picturesquely than by Nicholas and Queen Milena themselves. But the times are now hard and out of joint, a well-embroidered suit is expensive (and perhaps, after all, less practical in this material age than American reach-me-downs), there is no longer a Royal example for a loyal subject to follow, no longer a nation to stimulate a poor man or woman to make the necessary sacrifice on behalf of its traditions. When the Almighty, relates a Montenegrin legend, was passing over the face of the earth to distribute mountains, he dropped by mischance over Montenegro the sack containing all the rocks, so that the land was covered with the escaping boulders. From this grim, forbidding surface there is now vanishing its one gay patch of colour; and soon there will remain of one of the loveliest of national costumes nothing more than its single element of gloom, the cap whose mourning band recalls the national disaster on the field of Kossovo Polje over five hundred years ago.

The road built between 1876 and 1881 from Cattaro to Tsetinje is, with its formidable zigzags up the slopes of Mount Lovčen, one of the most remarkable in existence, just as the Bocche di Cattaro, in Croatian the Boka Kotorska, is the most remarkable fjord outside Norway. If I had to make a selection of the outstandingly beautiful drives in Europe, I should give a high place to that from Sorrento to Amalfi and an even higher to the road that follows the turns and twists of the Bocche from Cattaro to Castelnuovo (Ercegnovi). Cattaro itself, on the water's edge at the very head of the fjord with Lovčen rising with almost terrifying steepness immediately behind it, is a typical little town of the subject-lands of Venice, notwithstanding the fact that its population is partly Orthodox. It has both

a Catholic and an Orthodox cathedral, and in the former
is preserved, in a silver reliquary of exceptional interest
(Dalmatia generally is notable for its reliquaries), the
head of its patron saint, Tryphon. S. Tryphon was
martyred as a youth of eighteen under the Emperor
Decius and was brought to Cattaro for burial; and in
his memory was founded the still surviving guild of
seamen called in Italian the "Marinerezza" and in
Croatian the "Bokeljska Mornarica." In Venetian days
the guild was governed by an "admiral" who ranked
immediately after the Venetian Governor and wore a
uniform only a degree more picturesque than that of
the ordinary members: and, even now, on S. Tryphon's
day, the 3rd February, the historic dress of the guild
is worn in the procession which carries the head of the
Saint round the town and in the subsequent rejoicings,
after a lad, also arrayed in the uniform and known as the
"little admiral," has announced the advent of the feast
to the people in the presence of the civil and ecclesiastical authorities. But, alas, the Bocche are now dead
from the seafaring point of view, as witness the empty
and in many cases roofless and decaying palaces of the
towns that fringe the banks. Perzagno, Risano and
above all Pérasto are eloquent, in their handsome
Renaissance stone *palazzi*, of the former prosperity of
the Mediterranean sailing masters who congregated
in the Bocche; but, with the substitution of the steam-
ship for the sailing vessel, the families that built these
lordly houses are impoverished, their descendants are

168

PLATE VIII

Cattaro (Kotor) : Head of S. Tryphon.

Pérasto and the Bocche di Cattaro.

[To face p. 168.

struggling emigrants in the New World. Pérasto is the masterpiece of the group and rightly so, for the Pérastini were so renowned for their bravery and their loyalty to Venice that they were made the hereditary guardians of the banner of S. Mark, the Saint's *fedelissimi gonfalonieri*. Adorned with its two little islands of S. George and the Madonna of the Chisel (La Madonna del Scarpello), that guard, each with its church, the Bocche at their narrowest contraction, Pérasto is indeed a haunt of rare and forgotten beauty.

Immediately to the west of Castelnuovo the narrow valley of the Sutorina runs down to the entrance of the Bocche, thrusting, until the end of the Great War, a thin strip of Herzegovinan land across that of Dalmatia. The reason of this, as will appear below, was the desire of the Ragusan Republic to see a buffer of Turkish territory, if ever so narrow a one, between its own domain and that of the feared and hated Venice; and so we find ourselves, after crossing this valley, within the former confines of the Republic of S. Blaise.

III

THE REPUBLIC OF S. BLAISE

Probably few of those who recall that the 3rd February, in addition to being S. Tryphon's day, is also that of S. Blaise, are aware that the patron saint of woolcombers was also for many centuries the patron of the small but distinguished Republic of Ragusa, that his effigy appeared on the Ragusan coinage as late as the year 1805, that his banner, which the argosies of the said Republic in an earlier age carried not only the length of the Adriatic and the breadth of the Mediterranean but westward to the North Sea and eastward to the Indies, is flown in Ragusa even now on this day of the year from Orlando's Pillar in the Stradone. Not less close than the connexion of S. Mark with Venice is that of S. Blaise with her Dalmatian rival; his sturdy figure—coped, mitred, and fiercely bearded and moustachioed as befits a saint adopted by the Balkans—is as much in evidence on Ragusa's walls and gates as is S. Mark's lion in the territories of the late Serene Republic.

Ragusa—it is still a little difficult to think of her as Dubrovnik, the only name recognized by her new masters—has, however, more in common with Venice than the ubiquity of a patron saint. Both Republics were maritime states, and the Ragusan argosies (the word "argosy" is Ragusa's contribution to the English language) were almost as widely known in the Mediterranean as the Venetian galleys; Ragusan silver coins percolated the Levant (I have found one as far afield as Antioch) as freely as the gold ducat of Venice. In their buildings the resemblance is equally close: in a sense Ragusa may be described as a pallid yet not atrophied Venice. She is, of course, much smaller— *parva domus Ragusa sed sufficit orbi*, said one of her poets—and her population, now less than 10,000, probably never exceeded 35,000 even at the height of her fortunes; pallid she may be called in that the warm, living tones of the Venetian brick are replaced here by the dead whiteness of the Curzola stone. But this stone is capable of taking on with age a pale honey-coloured patina which has a rare beauty of its own; and its hard, clear, clean-cut effect saves Ragusa's occasional baroque churches from the decadent appearance of their Venetian contemporaries. Architecturally the influence of Venice is much in evidence: the Rector's Palace, now the King's, is the Doge's Palace in miniature; the Sponza or Dogana (the mint and custom house of the Republic) might but for its material be situated on the Grand Canal or the Piazzetta. But Ragusa boasts in her fortifications a feature which Venice perforce lacks, a superb and perfect cincture of wall, tower and bastion which places her on a level with Carcassonne and Aigues Mortes, with Avila, Rhodes and Famagusta, in the very front rank of cities walled by mediæval western military art. What is more, nothing within the walls does discredit to the city as seen from without. Despite the havoc wrought by the disastrous earthquake of the 6th April, 1667, the *dies iræ* of Rugusan history, much besides the Rector's Palace and the Sponza survived its ravages, notably the cloisters of the Franciscans and the Dominicans, who were brought to Ragusa early in the thirteenth century to check the spread of the Bogomile heresy and established themselves at the two ends of the city, the former just inside the Porta Pile, the latter by the Porta Ploče, being charged, as befitted the Church militant, with the defence of these two gates. The Stradone or Corso, Ragusa's main street, which was once a valley—indeed, a canal—whereby the city was bisected lengthways as was Jerusalem by the Tyropæum, was entirely destroyed, but it was rebuilt shortly afterwards in the traditional manner. Although its houses are uniform and each pair of them on the land side is separated by a narrow lateral street for greater security in future earthquakes, it is a stately thoroughfare, broad and airy, matching well the public buildings to which it leads and gaining dignity from the fact that no wheeled traffic can penetrate inside the walls. I am fortunate to have seen the Stradone at its best, namely, on the evening of a 6th April, when an annual procession commemorates the great disaster of 1667. On that day the Bishop of Ragusa, preceded by the Canons of the Cathedral and other clergy, by the Mayor and leading lay dignitaries of the city, carries the Host in solemn procession from the Gospa (Cathedral) to the little Church of S. Saviour by the Porta Pile (built by the Senate as a votive offering for the saving of the city during a previous earthquake in 1520) and back along the Stradone. The effect of the blue brocade baldaquin borne over the Bishop and the Host, of the vestments of the clergy, of the kneeling population, of the long tapers carried by those taking part in the procession, blending with the fading glow of the spring twilight in

PLATE IX

Ragusa : The Sponza.

Ragusa : The Rector's Palace.

[To face p. 172.

this singularly appropriate *décor*, make the scene one
of notable beauty. The symbol IHS carved on the
lintels of so many Ragusan houses is due to a pious
custom that arose after the earthquake of 1520.

While wholly western in her architecture, Ragusa
occupies in civilization and art a position midway
between western and eastern Europe, between Latin
and Slav, between Catholic and Orthodox. If the
political circumstances of the moment have brought
the Slav and Latin cultures into dissonance, even into
antagonism, Ragusa was able in the days of her independence to weld them into an harmonious whole.
This happy union was especially fruitful in poetry—
Italian in form and inspiration, Slavonic in language[1]
—which earned for Ragusa the title of "the Dalmatian
Athens" and gave her a place in letters no less distinguished than her place in the domains of navigation
and diplomacy. For the Ragusans were not only a race
of sailors, they were compelled by circumstances to be
astute diplomatists, combining here again, in their flexi-
bility tempered with the tenacity inspired by a strong
if narrow patriotism, something of both the Latin and
the Slav genius. The Ragusan ambassadors were not
the least effective of their country's servants, and this
in an age when the person of an envoy, especially in the
East, was not as sacred as it is now; on more than one
occasion it was their skill combined with constancy that

[1] *Cf.* J. Torbarina, *Italian Influence on the Poets of the Ragusan Republic*, London, 1931.

saved the little State from the hostile ambitions of Venice on the one hand, of the Turks on the other. There is now preserved in the Cathedral an object that appealed to me as one of the most characteristic relics of Ragusan history: it is a much-travelled Flemish triptych which accompanied all Ragusan missions to Constantinople to form the altar-piece of the Embassy chapel, whence it followed the luckless ambassadors and their staffs for prolonged periods to the Seven Towers.

Edmond Rostand has invented the verb *"raguser"* to describe the devious mentality (as exhibited at Essonne in 1814) of Marmont, created Duke of Ragusa by Napoleon in 1808; but the word might be applied not less appropriately to the diplomatic technique of the Republic. Forced by her smallness and her geographical position to live by her wits, Ragusa became politically during the sixteenth, seventeenth and eighteenth centuries a sort of intermediary between the Christian Powers and the Turks, in which position she learned to place more confidence in the latter, to whom for a long period she paid tribute,[1] than to the former as represented by Venice. If the reader will glance at a map of the Balkan peninsula of before 1919, he will see that the inland province of Herzegovina pushes two very narrow tentacles down to the sea, the one at Klek in the Canale di Narenta, the other, as we have seen, along the valley of the Sutorina into the Bocche

[1] For the last time in 1804.

di Cattaro. The enclave thus formed represented the
territory of the Ragusan Republic at its ultimate extent;
and it was at the instance of Ragusa, in her dislike of
the propinquity of Venice, that Turkey added the two
strips to the territory of Herzegovina in order to separate, if only by a few miles, the previously conterminous

frontiers of the two Republics. It is chronicled that the
insertion of the clauses in question into the Treaty of
Passarowitz owed not a little to the support of the
English Ambassador, urged thereto by his Ragusan
servant.

This episode, if true, is not Ragusa's only link with
England. Popular tradition ascribes the foundation of
her first Cathedral (the present Gospa was built after
the earthquake of 1667) to Richard Cœur de Lion, who,

narrowly escaping shipwreck off the islet of Lacroma on his return from the Third Crusade, vowed to build a church near the place of his delivery if he came safely to land. A link of another sort was provided by the Spanish Armada, in which the Ragusans, whose maritime connexion with Spain was a close one, lost twelve of their best fighting ships. Yet another link was forged towards the end of the Napoleonic wars, when the British Fleet added a chapter to Dalmatian history that began with the victory of Lissa in 1811. Between 1812 and 1815, when the whole of Dalmatia passed under the rule of Austria, the Ragusan islands were under British administration and experienced, as entrepôts of British goods then prohibited from entry into the mainland ports under French control, the most prosperous era they have known. In three years, for example, the population of Lissa rose from 4,000 to 12,000; and the commercial profits made by the Ragusan islanders while under the protection of the British flag exceeded those of the sunniest days of the Republic.

The Venetian Republic, as all the world knows, met her downfall at the hands of Bonaparte in 1797, but S. Blaise contrived to survive S. Mark for a full decade. He was, however, not less surely doomed: the State of Ragusa, albeit small, was not small enough to be spared by Napoleon "*comme échantillon de république*," as was little San Marino. It is true that as late as 1800 the constitution of Ragusa served as the model for that of the short-lived "Septinsular Republic" of the Ionian

Islands; nevertheless, on the last day of January, 1808, the representative of Marmont, French Commander-in-Chief in Dalmatia, summoned the Senate to assemble for the last time and, sitting beside the Rector, read out to it the laconic words: "the Republic of Ragusa has ceased to exist." It was characteristic of the two oligarchies of the Adriatic, Venice and Ragusa, that the hatred inspired by the ruling class—intensely jealous to the end of its exclusive privileges—in the rest of the population effectively mitigated the latter's grief at the loss of their independence. In Ragusa, on the night of Marmont's announcement, the burghers gave a ball to celebrate the end of the Republic, which they could only visualize at the moment as the end of the oligarchy. On the other hand, it is but fair to the oligarchy to recall that, on the loss of the Republic's independence, the aristocratic families entered into a voluntary compact of celibacy in order that they might die out, a compact which was faithfully carried out by all but two of the families concerned. So determined had been the Ragusan aristocracy to share its power with none that the Rector's term of office was fixed at one month, with the necessary consequence that his head on the coinage was a conventional one, in which nothing ever varied but the curls of the peruke. It is also easy to understand why in Ragusa's long history but a single Rector died in office—in the earthquake of 1667. During the period of Hungarian supremacy over Ragusa the Rectors received *ex officio* from the Kings of Hungary the Order of the Golden Spur; but it was only on their coffins that the relentless Senate allowed the insignia to be displayed.

If Ragusa could be hard to her sons, she has always enjoyed the reputation of protecting strangers in distress. This reputation is being maintained at the present day, for some 300 Russian refugees are now living there in safety, if in extreme poverty. They have had placed at their disposal a part of the *tête-de-pont* by the Porta Ploče, and within these massive fortifications have improvised dormitories, a reading-room and a rough-and-ready theatre, where they occasionally organize performances in aid of the most destitute among them. There is also a restaurant, managed by an old ex-Colonel and his wife, who do the cooking and serve the meals; and, although the appointments are of the most primitive, the company is good and there is a spirit about the place—a spirit of sadness and of courage withal—not usually associated with restaurants. It affords a contrast as striking as it is agreeable to the jazzing Prussian profiteers in the *Luxus-hotel* at the other end of the city, who seem singularly blind to the implications of Meštrović's plaque of King Peter of Yugoslavia (Ragusa's one striking modern work of art), which faces them from the walls of the Porta Pilé across the way.

PLATE X

Ragusa and the Island of Lacroma.

Plaque by Meštrovič of King Peter I of Yugoslavia on the Porta
Pilé, Ragusa.

[To face p. 178.

IV

Spálato and the Republic of Poljica

How many men who, when they come to retire, declare, with satisfaction or with bitterness as the case may be, that they are henceforth going to grow cabbages in their back garden, are aware that the first person to announce his withdrawal from public life in those particular terms was the Emperor Diocletian? But when the master of the western world explained how he proposed to employ his leisure after his abdication—he was the first Roman Emperor voluntarily to descend from the throne—it was with no bitterness, it was longingly and with real joy that he thought of the *olera manibus nostris insita*. Nor was this merely a passing whim. When his Imperial colleague Maximian, who cherished no similar ambitions and had shared in the abdication decidedly against his will, tried to persuade Diocletian that they should both return to power, the only reply he received was:

"If you only saw the cabbages planted by my own hand, you would never make so foolish a suggestion."

The important Roman city of the district in which Diocletian was born was the now ruined Salona, and it was to his own country that the Emperor decided to retire. Simple as were now his ambitions, however, it was not precisely a cottage that he proceeded to build for himself on a little peninsula some three miles south of Salona. Freeman calls Diocletian's Palace "the vastest

179

and noblest dwelling that ever rose at the bidding of a single man," and Horatio Brown admits that with its area of nine acres and a half it is a huge building for a single house. Even now it forms the nucleus of the town of Spálato and houses a considerable population both residential and industrial. Thus, for example, I have never had my hair cut in more satisfactory surroundings than in the excellent barber's shop in Diocletian's peristyle. Both the Palace, and Spálato as a whole, have been well and frequently described, and I do not propose to add another description here, especially as my main purpose is to say something of the Republic of Poljica, which is practically unknown. But as I also like to recall possibly unfamiliar English contacts, I would mention that in Diocletian's mausoleum, which is now one of the smallest and most perfect cathedrals in the world, there once presided in the seventeenth century as Archbishop of Spálato a prelate —one Mark Antony de Dominis—who in the course of a variegated career managed to be for a while an office-holder in the Church of England as Master of the Savoy and Dean of Windsor.

The leading authority on the antiquities of Salona and its neighbourhood is Mgr. Bulič, who conducted the excavations of both the pagan city and the early Christian necropolis. Realizing that ancient sites are not studied in the greatest comfort on an empty stomach, he also built an attractive little rest-house appropriately furnished, where visitors are regaled according to a Latin menu. *"Viator habes,"* announces the ·delightful bill of fare of this inn *"Ad Bonum Pastorem":*

VINUM SALONITANUM SIVE ALBUM SIVE
   RUBRUM SIVE NIGRUM OPTIMUM QUOD
   NON CORRUPIT MALITIA HOMINUM
ZYTHUM BOSNENSE VEL SLOVENICUM
AQUAM SALUBERRIMAM IADRI FLUMINIS
PERNAM SALONITANAM VEL CROATICAM VEL
   SLAVONICAM
CLUPEAS ISSAEAS SALSAS
OVA RECENTIA VEL SORBILIA VEL COCTA
BUTYRUM RECENS
CASEUM VEL DALMATICUM VEL BOSNENSEM
PANEM BIS COCTUM VEL DOMESTICUM
LAC VACCINUM
COGNAC SPALATINUM
MEL QUOD APIS TUSCULANA CONDIDIT
POTIONEM EX FABA ARABICA
FICUS · UVAM · PIRA · MELONES EX AGRO
   SALONITANO.

Could anything be more engaging, more encouraging than this? What if the *potio ex faba arabica* jumps a century or two, the *cognac Spalatinum* even more? Can we doubt that the wine of Salona, white or red, was not equally proof against the wickedness of man in the days of the Roman Empire; can anyone resist the appeal of the *mel quod apis Tusculana*—industrious insect—*condidit?*

To the west of Salona the rich, sheltered Riviera of the Sette Castelli—the Seven Castles—extends in a semicircle to Traù. The "Seven Castles" were fiefs granted by Venice to certain patrician families with the obligation to construct thereon castles for defence against the Turks, but have long since grown into prosperous and attractive seaside villages. And at the end of them, occupying a tiny islet wedged between the island of Bua and the mainland, is Traù or Trogir (in either case a dissyllable), architecturally a blend of Hungarian and Venetian Gothic and one of the most picturesque of mediæval towns to be found anywhere in Europe. I should like to linger over the beauties of Traù, over the thirteenth-century cathedral with its celebrated porch, over the ninth-century chapel of S. Barbara, the spacious Venetian Loggia, the narrow streets full of architectural gems, the astonishingly picturesque town walls and towers rendered yet more so by the surrounding water; but it is time to take the reader to the other side of Spálato, where begin the confines of what was surely the most obscure independent European State to survive into the nineteenth century.

Running southwards from behind Spálato is a mountain massif known as the Mossor, and between the Mossor and the sea is a lesser range, that of the Poljica. This range runs from the little bay of Stobreč, immediately to the east of Spálato, for some fourteen miles parallel with the coast to the town of Almissa, a place which earned during the Middle Ages an unsavoury reputation as a refuge of the pirates who arose with the break-up of the Roman Empire and infested the Adriatic for many centuries. The Poljica range forms the backbone of the small Republic of the same

PLATE XI

Three Views of Traù (Trogir).

Spálato (Split).

The Cathedral.

Entrance to the Iron Gate of
Diocletian's Palace.

To face p. 182.

name, which, claiming to have originated in the eleventh century, actually maintained an independent existence until swept away by Napoleon in 1807. The inland valley between the Poljica and

Mossor ranges forms the Upper Poljica, the Lower Poljica embraces the villages situated on the slope between the Poljica mountains and the sea. Originally consisting of ten villages, the Republic was enlarged in 1444 by the addition of Postrana and Jesenice, the gift

183

of Spálato, and henceforth embraced twelve villages
and their surrounding lands; and in 1806, the last
complete year of its independent existence, its population amounted to 6,566 souls, not counting the many
Poljicans settled in other parts of Dalmatia.

The Republic owes its traditional foundation to
three sons of the Bosnian King Miroslav, who are
believed to have migrated about the year 1015 to the
region of the Mossor. These Bosnians are supposed to
have been followed at no long interval by certain noble
Croatians from Hungary; and this much is certain, that
in later times the nobility of the little peasant Republic
was divided into two groups, that of the Bosnian and
that of the Hungarian or, rather, Croatian nobles. In
due course the growth of the community rendered
some form of constitutional organization necessary,
wherefore the Bosnian and Croatian nobles, probably
about the beginning of the fourteenth century, joined
in promulgating an organic law to determine the
government of the Republic. At the head of each
village there was placed a count (Croatian *Knez*,
Italian *Conte*), and every year on S. George's day, the
23rd April, the counts met with the nobles and the
non-nobles at the village of Gata to hold a general
assembly known as the *sbor*. At this *sbor* was chosen
the Great Count (*Veliki Knez, Conte Grande*), the
supreme head of the State, for the ensuing year, while
the local counts were also changed. The Great Count
was only eligible for re-election after an interval of

five years, but in later times this rule was generally waived and Great Counts have been known to be re-elected for as many as twenty consecutive years. The right of election was confined to the nobles (that of the Great Count to the Bosnian nobles alone), while the non-nobles were entitled to do no more than witness the elections. Thus it will be seen that Poljica was not a whit less an oligarchy than were her greater sisters Ragusa and Venice.

The Great Count enjoyed during his year of office the powers of a dictator, but, the year ended, had to give an account of his stewardship to the *sbor*. His official dress was one of considerable pomp: it consisted of a tall black velvet cap (*kalpak*) with gold fringes and a silver plume, a gold-laced purple robe with silver buttons, breeches in the Hungarian fashion and, over all, a scarlet mantle. He also carried a curved sword. During his year of office he had to visit each community of the Republic at least three times, accompanied by the four Procurators who assisted him in judicial matters.

In 1444 the Republic accepted the suzerainty of Venice and henceforth paid her an annual tribute of 3,000 Dalmatian lire (the equivalent of £25), while Venice also assumed the right to ratify the election of the Great Count. During the wars with the Turks the men of Poljica played an active part, despite the small-ness of their forces, in the Christian operations against the Moslem; and it fell to the French to put an end to the existence of this vigorous if unobtrusive little state. When in the Napoleonic wars France decided to suppress the Constitution of the Republic, the Poljicans turned to the Russians for help, whereupon Marmont made short work of them and from Gata issued a

Seal of the Republic of Poljica.

proclamation, in which he condemned the Great Count and most of the other office-holders of the Republic to be shot and ordered their property to be confiscated and their houses to be burned. This was in 1807. The last Great Count, Iovan Čovič, contrived to make his escape in a Russian ship and according to some

PLATE XII

Poljica : the Village of Dolac.

A descendant of one of the
Great Counts.

A Poljican House.

[To face p. 186.

accounts to take away with him the chest containing the charters and laws of the Republic. He reached Petrograd in safety and there ended his days in 1811, but Poljica as an independent state had ceased to exist.

To-day the Poljicans are scarcely to be distinguished from the other Slavs of the Dalmatian hinterland, although an Italian writer of half a century ago described them as "strong and inured to fatigue, mentally acute, sly to the point of malice, warlike and long-lived." Their former independence is no more than a memory, and they now confine their energies to their agricultural products, prominent among which is the bitter wild cherry—the *marasca*—that becomes of world-wide renown when transmuted into the maraschino and cherry-brandy of Zara.

V

THE ITALIAN ENCLAVES

At the division, after the War, of the Adriatic territories of the Austro-Hungarian Empire between Italy and what was then called the Kingdom of the Serbs, Croats and Slovenes, there was allotted to the former the Austrian Province of Istria; to the latter, with other regions, the Kingdom of Dalmatia, which had been Austrian, and the Banate of Croatia, which had been administered by Hungary. So far as the seaboard was concerned, this distribution meant that to Italy there fell, with the exception of Veglia, the islands belonging to Istria, namely, Cherso and Lussin with their adjacent

187

islets, while Yugoslavia acquired those attached to the
Dalmatian crown, extending from the supremely lovely
Arbe (now Rab), tucked away in the Quarnerolo well
to the north, even, of some of the Istrian islands, to the
frontier of Albania. But this division is subject to three

exceptions, for the Italians have acquired, as has been
said above, three strategic enclaves on the Albanian
and Dalmatian coasts. The island of Sáseno, which
overlooks and commands the spacious Albanian harbour
of Valona and may now be appropriately termed the
Gibraltar of the Adriatic, has already been mentioned;
the other enclaves, obtained under the Treaties of

188

Santa Margherita and Rapallo respectively, are the island of Lágosta, which was the westernmost of the possessions of the Ragusan Republic, and the town and district of Zara on the mainland. I am probably exceptional among travellers in having visited at one time or another all these three outposts of Italy in non-Italian lands, for, although Zara is comparatively well known and easily accessible, Sáseno is inhabited only by the Italian garrison and Lágosta has, apart from the Italian detachment, a population of barely more than a thousand. These are humble folk, mainly engaged in sardine and lobster fishing, but they still speak the Ragusan dialect, a mixture of pure Italian and pure Croatian.

The most interesting feature about Lágosta is an etymological one. Has Lágosta given its name to the carob or locust bean, which flourishes all over the island, or is it the tree that has christened the island? And whether Lágosta is locust, or locust has become Lágosta, there is the farther question whether the eponymous "locust" is the carob tree or the lobster, which with the crayfish (French *langouste*, Italian *aligusta*, *arigusta*) is as characteristic a product of the island as the carob bean. It may not be generally known that the English words "lobster" and "locust" are both derived from the same source, namely, the Latin *locusta*, and it is a remarkable circumstance that Lágosta should embody in its name its two principal but so divergent products.

189

At a supper-party one evening in Ragusa my neighbour mentioned in the course of conversation that she had spent the previous summer "in Italy." I asked where she had been, expecting some such answer as the Apennines or the Italian Lakes. To my surprise she answered: "Zara." Now Zara is as essentially Dalmatian a town as any along the eastern shore of the Adriatic, was, in fact, during the Austrian régime the capital of the Dalmatian Provincial administration; it was therefore interesting to find that Dalmatians think of a place in terms of its political allegiance even when that allegiance constitutes somewhat of a geographical anomaly. It was as if a Parisian lady of the fifteenth century had talked of paying a visit to England when she had in point of fact travelled no farther than Calais.

If the circumstance that Zara and its hinterland are now an integral part of the Italian kingdom may be said to constitute somewhat of a geographical anomaly, this is not to say that politically the fact is equally anomalous. Although the inhabitants of the neighbouring villages are, as are the villagers elsewhere in Dalmatia, Slavs in blood and in speech, the townsfolk are Italian-speaking and partly, at all events, of Italian, that is, Venetian, descent. And no less Venetian in physiognomy than most other towns of the Dalmatian littoral is the city where the Venetian Doge Enrico Dandolo deflected the course of the Fourth Crusade. The somewhat sordid story is too well known to need repetition here at any length; suffice it to recall that when the Crusaders began to assemble in Venice in the first year of the thirteenth century and found themselves unable to pay the Venetians the sums they had promised for their transport to the Holy Land, the Doge, a ruthless bargainer despite his blindness, agreed to forego the covenanted payment if the expedition would stop on its way to recover rebellious Zara for the Serene Republic. How this was done in 1202, how it was then decided at Zara to divert the Crusade from the expulsion of the Infidel from the Holy Places to the expulsion of the Christian—but only Orthodox— Emperor from Constantinople, how the New Rome was sacked by an army which had taken the Cross with a very different purpose and a Latin Emperor was set up for a while in place of the Greek, belongs to world history; but these fateful events gave Zara for a moment what to-day would be called "a front place in the news."

Zara occupies a peninsula joined to the mainland by a narrow isthmus, which was cut by the Venetians to convert the area occupied by the city into an island, but was subsequently filled in once more. The little peninsula runs almost north and south and on its western side looks across the beautiful Canale di Zara to the now Yugoslav island of Ugljan (Ugliano), dominated by the Venetian castle of S. Michael, on its eastern side across the Old Harbour to the mainland, to which it is joined by a recently constructed swing-bridge. The Lion of S. Mark is well in evidence on the city gates and elsewhere, as is Venetian influence in some of the later churches, notably in the little nuns' church of S. Maria, which is externally a replica of S. Maria dei Miracoli in Venice although internally a nightmare of rococo gone mad. The earlier Romanesque churches, on the other hand, have more in common with those of Lucca and Pisa. The cathedral, dedicated to S. Anastasia, is a noble basilica whose façade is not unworthy to be classed with that of the Duomo of Lucca, while its richly carved choir-stalls are in their different way a masterpiece of the Venetian wood-carver's art of the sixteenth century. Two yet more ancient buildings adjoin the cathedral: an hexagonal baptistery and the lofty circular ninth-century church of S. Donato—now used as a museum—which the architecturally sound if politically biassed Freeman describes as one of the noblest round churches in existence. The campanile was begun in the Romanesque style by the wealthy fifteenth-century Archbishop Valaresso, but was abandoned when the first storey was reached because the Archbishop's relatives succeeded in depriving him of the control of the family fortune. It was completed under the auspices of the Emperor Francis Joseph, who did so much for the preservation of Dalmatian antiquities, from the plans of Sir Thomas Jackson.

Similar in style to the Cathedral is the noble tri-apsidal Church of S. Chrysogonus. The Church of S. Simeon has been so defaced by the baroque plasterer as to be scarcely recognizable for what it is, a basilica of the twelfth century. But it deserves a visit for the sake of the magnificent silver shrine that houses the remains of the saint, bearing the date 1380 and an inscription giving as the donor the name of Queen Elizabeth of Hungary. The Church of the Franciscans should also be seen, partly for its fourteenth-century choir-stalls, partly for a pleasing Carpaccio (that amusing and delightful painter, if not actually by birth an Istrian or Dalmatian, was closely connected with the eastern coast of the Adriatic), partly for a large picture with predella of 1430, on a gold ground in the original frame, restored at the expense of the Emperor Francis Joseph.

VI

THE NOBLE COMMUNE OF TUROPOLJE

On the right bank of the Save, opposite the Croatian capital, Zagreb, lies a district unique in the world, the noble commune of Turopolje. This district, divided into twenty-two sub-districts and including in all thirty villages, contains a population of 13,000 souls, every one of whom, men, women and children, although peasants or, perhaps better, yeomen by descent and occupation, are at the same time noblemen and noblewomen by birth and have the right to display—and in point of fact do display—armorial bearings.

This rural community of Turopolje—the name is derived from *tur*, an aurochs, and *polje*, field—is the last surviving example of the tribal organizations characteristic of mediæval Croatia. The advent of feudalism tended to displace these tribal communities, so that even by the fourteenth century they had become reduced in numbers and by the seventeenth century had almost entirely disappeared. Turopolje, which first comes into notice in the thirteenth century, was fortunate to have merited the favour of King Albert IV of Hungary, who ennobled the entire community in recognition of some feat of arms. In 1560—by this time Turopolje had weathered the feudal menace to its continued existence—the members of the community drew up a new constitution which, despite many changes, forms the basis of that in force at the present time; and the final consolidation of their noble and autonomous status came in 1737, when the Emperor Charles VI, as King Charles III of Hungary, granted the community an official coat of arms which is in use to this day. Previously the authorities of the community had made use of their personal arms in sealing official documents, and it was with the object of introducing a more regular system that the Emperor decided that the district as a political entity should possess its communal coat. This achievement may be blazoned as follows:

"Azure upon a mount vert between two Croat soldiers gules, mantled, booted and bonneted argent, with mantles and bonnets trimmed with fur proper and holding in their exterior hands halberds argent, a

PLATE XIII

The Arms of Turopolje.

Headquarters of the Noble Commune of Turopolje at Velika Gorrica.

[To face p. 194.

tower of the last with steps leading to its gate proper and having two cannon or emerging from its embrasures. Upon the peak of the roof of the tower, gules, between three six-pointed stars dexter and a crescent moon sinister or a dexter arm embowed of the same holding a sabre proper."

Most of the individual families possess their own coats, which were either of their own original choice, subsequently confirmed by the rulers of Croatia, or given to them by direct Royal grant. They are all recorded and depicted in Laszowski's three-volume History of Turopolje, published at Zagreb in the Croatian language in 1910–24.

The head of the community is the Župan, who in accordance with the Statute of 1920 is elected for three years from among the qualified adult male members of the community. His salary is officially fixed at 2,500 dinars a month; but latterly the universal axe has forced its way even into this remote district and the Župan has to content himself for the present with a monthly emolument of only 2,300 dinars.

The Župan, who until 1918 occupied a seat *ex officio* in the Croatian Legislature, is assisted by twenty-four representatives of the individual sub-districts, and these dignitaries formerly exercised magisterial and judicial functions in their respective villages. But the administrative reforms introduced by the Central Government in the nineteenth century gradually withdrew the autonomous legal jurisdiction of the community, leaving to it as its principal remaining attribute the control of its considerable landed property. This communally owned landed property consists of some 16,000 acres of agricultural and forest land, which is administered for the joint benefit of the community. The distribution of the arable land, the pasturage, the wood fuel, the acorns from the oak forests for the pigs, *et cetera*, is minutely regulated, is confined to membership of the noble community, and is linked with the ownership of a manor or part of a manor. There are some 700 of these manors in Turopolje, but they are capable of subdivision by inheritance, so that there are cases of individuals possessing only one 120th share of a manorial right. The capital of the commune is the village of Velika Gorica, where, in a building adorned with the arms of Turopolje, the chosen representatives of this peasant aristocracy continue to administer what remains to them of their ancient and singular privileges.

SOME VISITORS FROM THE EAST TO THE PLANTAGENET AND LANCASTRIAN KINGS

VIII

SOME VISITORS FROM THE EAST TO THE PLANTAGENET AND LANCASTRIAN KINGS

In the thirteenth and fourteenth centuries the British Isles represented to the dwellers in the East the Ultima Thule of the known world, and few and far between were the Oriental visitors of the period who penetrated to our remote and forbidding shores. Nevertheless, the leading part played by English kings in the Crusades, the contact so strangely established between Edward I and certain rulers of the Mongols by a mutual hatred of the Saracen, the need of western help against the growing menace of the Turks felt by the eastern outposts of Christendom, led sundry emissaries from the East to seek the presence of the westernmost of the sovereigns of Europe. The five visitors, of whom I propose here to tell, have only one factor in common, namely, that the object of their visits was the same: to seek the aid of the English King against the armies of Islam. In other respects they show a singular diversity. Three were the envoys of a king; two were themselves crowned heads. One was Catholic and by race a Frank, one was Orthodox and a Greek, one a

Genoese established in Central Asia, one a Tatar converted to Christianity, one a Mongol born a Nestorian Christian in Peking. It is with the last mentioned that I will begin my narrative.

In 1227 there died the Mongol conqueror Jenghiz, who, by birth the son of a petty Central Asian chieftain, had built up an Empire that extended at the time of his death from the China Sea to the Crimea. Of this Empire Jenghiz was the first Khakan (Great Khan), the supreme overlord, under whom individual provinces were governed, with varying degrees of autonomy, by feudatory Khans of his family. In 1251 one of his grandsons, Hulagu, the conqueror of Baghdad, established in Persia, subject to the suzerainty of the Khakan in Peking, the dynasty of the Il-Khans, which endured for the ensuing century; and it is with a grandson of Hulagu, Argon, who reigned in Persia and Mesopotamia as the fourth Il-Khan from 1284 to 1291, that we are for the moment concerned.

One of the outstanding and perhaps most surprising characteristics of the princes of the House of Jenghiz was their tolerance in matters of religion. Nominally Shamanists as were the earlier Mongol sovereigns, they were equally friendly to Christianity, Buddhism and Islam. It was not until the Empire of Jenghiz and Kublai fell to pieces from sheer unwieldiness that the rulers of its component parts gravitated definitely towards Islam in the West, Buddhism in the East. If they showed favour to one faith more than to another in this earlier period they did so towards Christianity. They took to wife not only Mongol ladies belonging to Nestorian Christian tribes but even Byzantine princesses; sometimes they allowed their children to be baptized; while they sought on several occasions to enter into political relations with Christendom, seeing in the Pope and the temporal rulers of Europe possible allies against their principal western enemies, the Arab Khalifate, the Egyptian Mamluks and the Empire of the Seljuq Turks. One of those most favourable to Christianity and most eager for an alliance with the Christian West was the Il-Khan Argon, whose three embassies to the Court of Edward I form the subject of the first part of this chapter.

The story of the earliest of these embassies is told in one of the most curious manuscripts that have come down to us from the Middle Ages—one of the most curious because, true counterpart of the narratives of Marco Polo and his European contemporaries, it relates the experiences of a Mongol Christian, a native of Peking, in the course of his travels from his birthplace overland to the remote West. I will not recapitulate here the beginning of the story, which is concerned with the birth, parentage and upbringing of two native members of the Nestorian Church in China, Mark and Bar-soma, both Uighurs by race, of their determination to enter the monastic life and the priesthood and to make the pilgrimage from their distant Chinese home to the Holy Places of Palestine, of the vicissitudes of their long and dangerous journey across Asia. Suffice it to say that Mark ultimately finds himself elected Patriarch of the Nestorian Church under the name of Yahb-Allaha III and, instead of returning to his native land, remains at the seat of the Patriarchate in Mesopotamia with his friend Bar-soma at his side.

Six years after Yahb-Allaha's consecration Argon determines to enter into negotiations with the Pope and the princes of Europe for an alliance against the Egyptian Mamluks, and he asks the Patriarch, with whom he is on friendly terms, to find him a suitable envoy. Yahb-Allaha nominates Bar-soma, a choice particularly agreeable to Argon, who believes the despatch as his ambassador of a real Mongol Christian of high rank, the intimate friend of the Patriarch of Eastern Christendom, to be well calculated to convert to his views the Pope and the Frankish kings. Accompanied by an appropriate retinue and entrusted with letters and presents to the potentates to whose Courts he is being despatched, Bar-soma sets out on his mission in 1287, supplied with "thirty excellent mounts and 2,000 *mithqals* of gold." The manuscript now proceeds to describe in detail the successive stages of his journey, first to the shores of the Black Sea and thence to Constantinople, where he is welcomed by the Byzantine Emperor, Andronicus II. This Emperor, whom the author of the manuscript calls Basil, mistaking his title *Basileus* for his name, was connected with the Mongols through the marriage of one of his daughters to the ruler of the Golden Horde, and receives the envoy with great friendliness, placing at his disposal as a residence what would now be described in Constantinople as a *khan*. Having inspected the sights and shrines of Byzantium, Bar-soma obtains the Emperor's leave to proceed on his way in order to comply with the orders of King Argon "to penetrate among the Franks," takes ship to Italy, sees Stromboli in eruption, and from the terrace of a house in Naples witnesses a naval battle between *Irid Kharladu* (the author's version of the name of the King of Naples, "il re Carlo due") and *Irid Arkun* ("il re d'Aragon"). After this introduction to European politics our envoy proceeds to Rome, where he learns that the Pope (Honorius IV) is dead, but he is conducted into the presence of twelve great lords called *Kardinale*, assembled in conclave to elect a new Pope; to these he expounds the nature of his mission as well as the Nestorian confession of faith. Since, however, there is for the moment no Pope with whom he can discuss the business of his embassy, Bar-soma proceeds to the other States to which he is accredited, beginning with Genoa, where he sees the Holy Grail, taken by the Crusaders at the capture of Cæsarea in Palestine in 1101. His next visit is to the King of France, Philip IV, who orders his "emirs" to show the envoy the sights of Paris, and then follows that part of his embassy which is of special interest to us, namely, his visit to "King *Alangitar* in *Kasonia*." The author of the manuscript, or a copyist, has here again mistaken, as is his habit, the title for the personal name, for this mysterious personage is none other than the King of "Angleterre," Edward I, then visiting his province of Gascony. Twenty days after leaving Paris Bar-soma reaches "the town"—no doubt Bordeaux—where the King is in residence, and is received by Edward with enthusiasm upon his unfolding his master's proposals for a simultaneous invasion of the Holy Land from east and west. "We, the kings of these regions," declares Edward, "have placed the emblem of the Cross upon our bodies, and have no preoccupation greater than this [sc. the recapture of Jerusalem]. My heart rejoices to learn that what I long for, King Argon desires also."

The King then receives, at his own request, the Holy Communion at the hands of this Nestorian from Peking, whom he sends on his way with gifts and with a favourable answer to the invitation of his master. Bar-soma, having thus no need to cross the Channel, now revisits Rome to negotiate with Nicholas IV, the Pope elected during his absence, and returns home towards the end of 1288.

In the hope of converting from words into deeds the offers of co-operation brought back by Bar-soma, Argon, in 1289, decides to despatch another embassy to the Pope and to the Kings of France and England, and on this occasion selects as his envoy not only a Christian but a European in the person of one Buscarel, a Genoese of whose previous history little is known.

Leaving Persia after the Easter of 1289, Buscarel presented himself in the first instance to the Pope, who from Rieti on the 30th September of that year addressed a Bull to Edward; in this Bull Nicholas requested the King to receive kindly the noble Genoese, *Biscarellus de Gisulfo*, and to give careful ear to the message he would deliver from Argon, the illustrious King of the Tatars. We have few details of the incidents of the voyage, but we know that on the Eve of the Epiphany, the 5th January, 1290, Buscarel arrived in London, accompanied by three gentlemen, a cook, eight horsemen and six domestics. Remaining in England twenty days, thirteen of which were spent at Court, he presented his letters from Argon and the Pope, and was received with great friendliness by the King, who defrayed from his own purse the mission's entire expenses. When Buscarel recrossed the Channel it was as the bearer of a letter from Edward to Argon, in which the English King expressed his intention to lead an army against the Sultan of Babylon (*i.e.* Egypt) as soon as he had obtained the Pope's concurrence. It is curious to note the modern sound of his form of address to Argon: "Your Royal Highness—*vestra regia celsitudo*," but he was in keeping with his times in his promise to send by special messengers a consignment of falcons for which the Il-Khan had asked.

The Pope, more than anxious to take advantage of the proffered Mongol help, was urgent that Edward should keep his promise, but Edward, whilst full of good intentions, was immobilized in Britain by his wars with the Scots. Thus was Argon twice disappointed of his hopes, but he made yet another attempt to organize the campaign he had at heart, and in 1290 despatched a third embassy to the Pope and the King of England, under the leadership of one Chagan, a converted Tatar. Chagan, who had adopted the baptismal name of Andrew on his conversion, was evidently a personage of importance, since the previous plenipotentiary, Buscarel, was now a member of his suite and only figures as the second name on the list of his staff. The details of Chagan's stay in England are not preserved, but the mission remained in the West sufficiently long to learn in Rome of the capture of Acre, the last outpost of the Crusaders in the Holy Land, by the Mamluk Melek al-Ashraf in May, 1291. The news caused something like consternation in Europe, and the Pope now redoubled his efforts to give tangible effect to the Il-Khan's proposals. But Argon did not live to see the return of his ambassador, for he had died on the 7th March of that year. While we have the text of the Pope's letters by Chagan, we do not know the nature of Edward's answer; more than ten years later, however, in March, 1302, he wrote to one of Argon's sons, Kazan, then reigning as the seventh Il-Khan, and to the Patriarch Yahb-Allaha, to excuse and explain his failure to lead an army to Palestine. Accompanying Edward's envoy, one Geoffrey de Langles, we meet once again our old friend Buscarel, who joined the party in his native Genoa and there helped the English mission to buy their requirements for the journey. That they equipped themselves on a generous scale may be inferred from the sum of £193 12s. 7d., a heavy amount in those days, which they expended on silver plate, £44 5s. on crockery and accoutrements, and £15 15s. 6d. on the fifteen carpets which they used as beds. Less extravagant was the outlay of 2s. on two "parasols," bought at Trebizond and Tabriz respectively. On the conclusion of their mission the envoys returned to England with a caged leopard, fed during the voyage on sheep carried from Constantinople for the purpose.

We will now pass to the reign of Edward III and to the visit to his Court of the King who may justly be called the greatest knight-errant the world has seen, King Peter I of the Lusignan dynasty that reigned in Cyprus from 1192 to 1489. The Latin kingdom of Cyprus was in truth a prolongation of the crusading kingdom of Jerusalem. On the execution of the luckless Conradin in 1268 the title of King of Jerusalem, together with the meagre remnants of the kingdom, passed to the kings of Cyprus; and, after the fall of Acre, the kings and queens of Cyprus received the crown of Jerusalem at Famagusta as being the Cypriote town geographically the nearest to the lost kingdom, the reconquest of which was henceforth their prevailing ambition. By none of these princes was the ambition more passionately cherished than by Peter I, who reigned from 1359 to 1369 but was vowed, even from the days before his accession, when he was still Count of Tripoli, to a perpetual Crusade against the Saracens. Peter commemorated his vow in his Order of the Sword, whose motto was *"pour loyauté maintenir"*; and it is recorded that he kept a naked sword constantly suspended from his neck in memory of his oath. Whatever be the truth of this story, it is at all events the case that of all the kings and queens of Cyprus he is the only one to be depicted on the coinage holding a sword instead of a sceptre.

This Peter, then, filled with Crusading ardour, twice went the round of the Courts of Europe to collect men and money for the recovery of the Holy Land. In 1362 he set out on the first of his journeys to the rulers of Christendom and, after visiting the Pope, the Emperor and the King of France, crossed the Channel to enlist the aid of the kings of England and Scotland. He was helped in his quest by his handsome appearance, his courtly manners, his gallant demeanour and his skill in all knightly accomplishments; and Froissart, to whom we are primarily indebted for our detailed knowledge of Peter's Odysseys, calls him "a man of excellent understanding, master of many languages, and much beloved." It was in 1364 that King Peter, after waiting in Calais for twelve days for a favourable wind, crossed the Channel and landed at Dover, where he remained two days while his ship was unloaded and his horses were disembarked. He then travelled by

easy day-journeys to London, where he was honour-
ably received not only by the British Lords sent by
Edward to meet him, but also by several Barons of
France, then held as hostages in England.

"It would take me a day," relates Froissart, "were I
to attempt relating to you the grand dinners, suppers,
and other feasts and entertainments that were made, and
the magnificent presents, gifts and jewels which were
given, especially by Queen Philippa, to the accomplished King of Cyprus. In truth, he was deserving of
them, for he had come a long way and at a great
expense to visit them, to exhort the King to put on
the red cross and assist in regaining countries now
occupied by the enemies of God. But the King of
England politely and wisely excused himself, by say-
ing: 'Certainly, my good cousin, I have every inclination to undertake this expedition; but I am growing too
old, and shall leave it to my children. I make no doubt,
that when it shall have been begun, you will not be
alone, but will be followed most willingly by my knights
and squires.' 'Sir,' replied the King of Cyprus, 'what
you say satisfies me. I verily believe they will come,
in order to serve God and do good to themselves; but
you must grant them permission so to do; for the
knights of your country are eager in such expeditions.'
'Yes,' answered the King of England; 'I will never
oppose such a work, unless some things should happen
to me or to my kingdom which I do not at this moment
foresee.' The King of Cyprus could never obtain

anything more from King Edward, in respect to this croisade; but, as long as he remained, he was politely and honourably feasted with a variety of grand suppers.

"About this time King David of Scotland had some affairs to transact with King Edward that made it necessary for him to come to England; so that when he heard the King of Cyprus was there, he hastened his journey in order to meet him, and made such despatch that he arrived in London before he had left it. The two kings were much rejoiced to meet, and congratulated each other upon it. The King of England gave them two grand entertainments in his palace of Westminster. At the last of these, the King of Cyprus took his leave of the King and Queen of England, who made him very magnificent presents: King Edward gave him also a ship called the Katharine, which was very beautiful and well built. The King of England had had her constructed, by his orders, to make the voyage to Jerusalem. She was valued at twelve thousand francs, and lay in the harbour of Sandwich."

Not by Edward alone was Peter feasted in London, for, like royal visitors of a later age, he was dined by the Mayor of the City; one of the historical paintings in the Royal Exchange depicts the celebrated banquet at which the Kings of England, Scotland, France and Denmark were King Peter's fellow-guests. Stow, in his Chronicle, gives us the following account of this entertainment, which appears to have lived long in the memories of the citizens of London:

"Henry Picard, vintner, Mayor of London, in one day did sumptuously feast Edward King of England, John King of France, the King of Cyprus (then newly arrived in England), David King of Scots, Edward Prince of Wales, with many noblemen and others: and after, the said Henry Picard kept his hall against all comers whosoever that were willing to play at dice and hazard. In like manner, the Lady Margaret, his wife, did also keep her chamber to the same intent. The King of Cyprus, playing with Henry Picard in his hall, did win of him fifty marks; but Henry being very skilful in that art, altering his hand, did after win of the said king the same fifty marks and fifty marks more; which when the said king began to take in ill part, although he dissembled the same, Henry said unto him, 'My lord and king, be not aggrieved: I covet not your gold, but your play; for I have not bid you hither that I might grieve you, but that amongst other things I might try your play;' and gave him his money again, plentifully bestowing his own amongst the retinue. Besides, he gave many rich gifts to the King and other nobles and knights, who dined with him, to the great glory of the citizens of London in those days."

Returning to the East after an absence of nearly three years, Peter swooped down upon Egypt, the stronghold of Arab power, and by a brilliant *tour de main* seized Alexandria, although he held it for only one day. Again he went on his travels, undeterred by the ephemeral nature of his triumph, but was recalled by troubles in Cyprus. In 1369, after a reign of ten years filled with a variety of picturesque and tragic incident with which the history of the Middle Ages affords no parallel, he was stabbed to death by some of his nobles, and with Peter died the hopes of the last Crusade. Not wholly undeserved is Chaucer's kindly judgment on the gallant and ill-fated King, whose visit to Edward III brought to England something of the glamour of his romantic island kingdom:

> "O worthy Petro, King of Cypre, also,
> That Alisaundre wan by heigh maistrye,
> Ful many a hethen wroghtes tow ful wo,
> Of which thyn owene liges hadde envye,
> And, for no thing but for thy chivalrye,
> They in thy bedde han slayn thee by the morwe.
> Thus can fortune hir wheel governe and gye,
> And out of Ioye bring men to sorwe."

The last of the five visitors was the only one in the long list of Byzantine Emperors to penetrate to the British Isles. In 1391 Manuel Palæologus, being then a prisoner in the hands of the Ottoman Sultan Bayazid I, the terrible "Yildirim" (Thunderbolt), succeeded to the perilous inheritance of his father, the Emperor John V, and had to escape from Brusa in order to ascend a throne that was already tottering before the pressure and blows of the Turks. Little more than Constantinople and the Peloponnese remained to the Eastern Emperors of their former territories, and the Turk was drawing ever closer the ring of ships and armies that was gradually encircling the coveted capital.

PLATE XIV

[*Photograph by Henry Dixon and Son, Ltd.*

The Master Vintner as Lord Mayor of London entertains Edward III,
Peter I of Cyprus and three other Kings.

*From the late Chevallier Tayler's picture in the Royal Exchange. King Peter's shield is
the second from the left. By permission of the Gresham Committee.*

[*To face p.* 212.

An attempt to relieve the pressure with western support resulted in a crushing defeat of the Christian forces by Bayazid at Nicopolis on the Danube in 1396, and Manuel's situation was well-nigh desperate when he decided in 1399 to make a personal appeal to the kings of the West for farther succour in his plight.

On the 10th December, 1399, Manuel set sail from Constantinople in Venetian galleys, breaking his journey in the Peloponnese in order to leave his wife, the Empress Irene, and his three young sons in the care of his brother Theodore, Despot of the Morea. He then proceeded to Venice, where he was received in state by the Doge and the Senate, was lavishly entertained and was promised material aid against the common enemy. The Italian chroniclers of the time make many references to the Imperial visitor, whom they call Chiriamomolle, a corruption of Κὺρ Μανουήλ, the Lord Manuel.

His sojourn in Venice at an end, the Emperor passed on to Padua and Pavia, being treated with all honour by the Carrara and the Visconti, and then crossed the Alps into France, where, but for his visit to England, he spent the ensuing two and a half years. The French King, Charles VI, had recently recovered from one of his attacks of madness and gave, together with his family and his Court, a warm welcome to his august but unfortunate guest. Manuel's well proportioned and impressive stature, his noble mien and bodily activity, his superb horsemanship which belied the

213

long hair and beard, both prematurely whitened by
misfortune, impressed themselves deeply upon the
imagination of the Parisians, who were astonished to
see the venerable Sovereign vault with the agility of a
youth, without setting foot on the ground, from the
horse which had carried him from the Bridge of
Charenton to the back of the white charger that awaited
him, a particular honour, at the gates of Paris.

It may be well to recall here how it came about that
this monarch in distress, without lands, without money,
without troops, without resources, with the mere
shadow of power, was yet able, an itinerant beggar, to
command the respect, indeed the veneration which was
enjoyed by the greatest and most powerful of his predecessors. Not even the long tale of defeats and other
humiliations had served to kill the awe which was felt
by mediæval Europe for the sacrosanct character of
the Byzantine Emperor. The Basileus of Constantinople had always embodied in its completest form the
monarchical conceptions of Christendom: the heir to
the authority and traditions of the Cæsars, he was not
only the final legislator and the supreme military commander of his people; he was the elect and anointed of
God, the head and defender of the Christian religion,
the equal of the Apostles. He was king and priest alike,
infallible both in temporal and in spiritual affairs; and
he exacted and received the most Oriental forms of
submission from his subjects, who approached his
person in the attitude of adoration and were content to

style themselves his slaves. Thus, not even the misfortunes which had left the once glorious Eastern Empire but a maimed torso had extinguished the tradition of majesty built up in more prosperous centuries; and men still regarded Manuel, even on his humiliating errand, as the Lord's anointed and the personification of Imperial Rome.

Manuel rapidly endeared himself to the Parisians. He was an honoured guest at the important social events of the day. He hunted and he visited churches (having an especial affection for the Abbey of S. Denis), while to attend his private chapel, where the liturgy was celebrated for him according to the Byzantine rite, became one of the fashionable pastimes of society in the French capital, to whom the icons and the eastern ceremonial afforded an interesting novelty. All was going well when King Charles's health suffered a relapse; and it was doubtless this circumstance which led Manuel to visit England, at a season unpropitious both politically and climatically. For it was little more than a year since Henry IV had seized the crown from the unfortunate Richard II (who met his end in the very year of the visit), while the Channel crossing on that 11th day of December, 1400, was evidently a rough one. Landing at Dover and thence proceeding through Kent, Manuel was well received at Canterbury by the Austin Friars, and on the 21st December, the feast of S. Thomas, was met at Blackheath by Henry. From Blackheath the two Sovereigns made their entry in procession into London, and both there and subsequently at Eltham, where he spent Christmas, Manuel was entertained in a manner which evoked his warm appreciation.

"The Prince with whom we are now residing," he writes to his friend Manuel Chrysoloras in Constantinople (the Emperor added to his other qualities a wide range of intellectual interests and considerable gifts of literary expression), "the King of Great Britain—a country which may be called a veritable other world—this Prince of great substance, embellished with a thousand great qualities, adored even by those who do not know him and causing those who have seen him but once to say that Fame, losing her divine power, is unable to celebrate such merit; this Prince, I say, illustrious in rank, illustrious in mind, who can deal a hard blow but also knows how to win friends with prudence, who holds out to everyone a helping hand, offering himself as a universal protector to all who have need of protection, has followed his natural inclination in becoming for us a haven after a double tempest, the one of nature, the other of fortune. His speech is full of charm; he delights us in every way, honours and loves us equally. His only fear is that what he does for us is not enough, and he seems on this account to blush, so magnanimous is he. He will give us help in men-at-arms, in archers, in money and in ships, which will convey the troops whithersoever it be necessary."

Alas that Henry failed to justify this somewhat fulsome praise. Accepting at their face value Henry's assurances, Manuel returned in February, 1401, to Paris, whence he wrote to his friends in Constantinople that his plans for the expedition to be fitted out by the French and English Kings were maturing so well that he hoped soon to be returning in its wake to his dominions. Unhappily Charles VI now suffered another return of his malady. While Manuel lingered impotently in France, waiting for Henry's promises to materialize, the French were too distracted by the struggle between the Dukes of Burgundy and Orleans for the control of the kingdom to give much thought to the luckless Greek. And then, suddenly, salvation came whence it was least expected, from the East. The Mongol Timur the Lame, that greatest of all human destroyers of men, had burst, himself a rebel against the House of Jenghiz, out of Central Asia and, at the battle-field of Angora in July, 1402, brought the advance of the Ottomans for the time being to a standstill. The terrible Yildirim was a prisoner in the hands of the yet more terrible Tamerlane, to die in captivity a few months later. Manuel now hastened back to his capital, the richer only by a few galleys, sundry presents and happy recollections; but his Empire had received, as if by a miracle, a respite of half a century before it met its end under the heroic leadership of the last Constantine, Manuel's youngest son.

AQABA

IX

AQABA

WHERE FOUR COUNTRIES MEET

IN 1892 Abbas Hilmi, the last Khedive, succeeded to an inheritance reduced in one respect from that of his predecessors. The Ottoman *firman* whereby his Imperial suzerain invested him with the Pashalik of Egypt omitted mention of the Sinai Peninsula and certain posts on the eastern side of the Gulf of Aqaba which had been administered by Mohammed Ali and the five rulers who followed him, and thus sought to exclude Egypt from the administration of any territory east of the Suez Canal. Under pressure from Great Britain the Sultan modified his attitude by recognizing the *status quo* in Sinai itself, while resuming possession of the posts on the eastern side of the Gulf hitherto garrisoned by Egypt. Great Britain agreed to this course and the Turco-Egyptian frontier was accepted (although the Turks successfully resisted delimitation) as running south-eastward from Rafa on the Mediterranean to the head of the Gulf of Aqaba; and this was the position until 1906, when mutual accusations by Turks and Egyptians of encroachments upon each other's territory decided the Egyptian Government to occupy the small port of Taba on the western side of the Gulf. Before this force could reach its destination Taba was seized by the Turkish Commandant at Aqaba and a situation of severe tension followed, ending in a British ultimatum to the Sultan to evacuate Taba within ten days. The Turks offered a compromise which, had it been accepted, would have added, as events have turned out, the eastern half of the peninsula to the Palestine of the Mandate; but Lord Cromer and the British Government remained firm. On the tenth day Abdul Hamid yielded, and agreed that the frontier should be formally delimited to run from Rafa to a point on the Gulf of Aqaba not less than three miles to the west of that town.

Two tracks converge upon this outpost of many nations and dynasties, forgotten by the modern world until the diplomatic incident summarized above brought it again into a brief prominence. One, from the west, is the pilgrimage route across the Sinai Peninsula to Mecca, along which the Faithful from Moslem lands westward of the Holy Cities toiled for the centuries that intervened between the institution of the *haj* and the construction of the Hejaz Railway. Although at present the railway does not operate south of Ma'an, the Sinai route has not yet come into its own again: the pilgrims that follow it are rare birds, and few people now traverse it beyond an occasional enterprising traveller in an agile American car. The other route is from the north, dotted with Roman milestones but probably older than Roman times, leading southward from Ma'an to the Aila which the famous Tenth Legion held in the teeth of the Beduin of Arabia Petræa. This route is likewise passable for cars of tried endurance, has indeed for some thirty miles south of Ma'an, thanks to the Public Works Department of the Transjordan Government, pretensions to being a dry-weather road. Then, at Naqb al-Ashtar, the great Syrian plateau that extends eastwards to Iraq falls abruptly away. The limestone ends in a vast ring of cliffs that drop a sheer 3,000 feet or so to a flat sandy bottom; and from the floor of the gigantic circle bounded by the limestone walls, which is known as the plain of Khizmeh, there rise fantastically shaped mountains of sandstone of the same brilliant colouring—purple, deep red, pink and ranging thence to saffron and pale yellow—as that of Petra. Indeed, I believe that had the Nabatæans established the entrepôt of their caravan trade and their necropolis here instead of in the Wadi Musa, they would have found in the Khizmeh an even more amazing *décor* for their habitations and their art.

About half-way across this circle is the police post of al-Ghuweira, whence Lawrence marched in September, 1917, through the Wadi Rûm, by a track that we followed on our return from Aqaba, to the Hejaz Railway Station of Mudawwara. Near the post we found, scratched on a ledge of one of those great masses of red sandstone that rise sheer from the level floor of the circle, some inscriptions in the early Arabic script called Safaitic, accompanied by lifelike pictographs of ibexes, dogs, an unmistakable wolf or two and camels with the hooded litters in which Arabian ladies were wont to travel even in pre-Islamic times and modern irreverence bluntly but expressively terms "bint-boxes." Incidentally I may record that in the old stone fort at Mudawwara, one of those places of refuge for pilgrims which punctuate the *haj* road from Damascus, we found a family of Beduin who spoke eagerly and with personal knowledge of "al-Uruns." [1]

At the southern end of the Khizmeh the configuration of the land again changes completely. We come now to a confused mass of granite, tortured and twisted into jagged peaks such as one supposes the mountains of the moon to be, into ridges serrated as sharply as the edge of a saw, their streaks of brown and green strata turned on end by some powerful and primeval convulsion of nature. Through this nightmare region the Wadi 'Atm vents itself into the Gulf of Aqaba, so narrow that little sun penetrates between the sheer naked granite walls on either side, and well named the "Valley of Darkness." Alone the Roman milestones, and an occasional Kufic inscription or Bedu *wasm* (tribal symbol) scratched on a rock, serve as a reminder that this wild and sinister pass has been for no inconsiderable period a human highway.

It was with relief that we emerged upon the blue

[1] One of the Arabic versions of the name "Lawrence."

waters of the head of the Gulf, even though the Gulf's
rugged and all but uninhabited shores give it an air of
melancholy, almost of grimness, and Aqaba itself is
reduced to a mud village of 150 souls. No longer an
entrepôt of trade and the pilgrim traffic, it now houses

a few apathetic fisher-folk; and a half ruined Mamluk
fort, an unpretentious *sarai* and a fairly extensive grove
of date palms alone now speak of a more prosperous
past. To-day its main interest is that of a territorial
curiosity, for upon some five miles of coast-line, of
which Aqaba village is approximately the centre, the
boundaries of four states converge. The frontier between Egypt and Palestine runs, as has been said, into

P   225

the Gulf at a point three miles to the west of Aqaba town, whence Palestine has about two miles of coast-line—its only outlet to the Red Sea—until the thalweg of the Wadi Araba marks the beginning of the Emirate of Transjordan. To Transjordan belong the next three miles or so, including Aqaba itself, and then begin, two miles below Aqaba, the dominions of Ibn Saud and we are politically in the real Arabia.

Here was the Eloth of the Book of the Kings, and beside it the Ezion Geber, "the Giant's Backbone" (an allusion, perhaps, to the spiny ridges of the granite hills behind it), where Solomon built a navy and despatched it, manned by the seamen of King Hiram, to Ophir for gold. The principal seat of the maritime trade of the Edomites and Israelites, Eloth became in Roman times the Aila of Arabia Petræa, garrisoned by that Tenth Legion whose traces are not yet wholly obliterated, and subsequently the Ailah of the pre-Crusading Arab geographers, in whose time it was still an important centre of commerce. But the most picturesque period in Aqaba's long history was when, as Ailat, it became one of the most audacious of all the fortresses of the Crusaders and, as the southernmost outpost, not only of the Principality of Oultre-Jourdain but of Crusading effort in general, was the scene of *gesta dei per francos* which amazed even that generation, which was not easily surprised. In 1116 the Crusaders had possessed themselves of Ailat and its adjacent island fortress of Graye, but had lost them again to Saladin in 1175.

Renaud of Châtillon, Prince of Oultre-Jourdain, that tempestuous and much perjured *preux* who was perhaps, with all his faults, the most redoubtable and determined figure thrown up on the Christian side by the Crusades, conceived the plan, fantastic in its boldness, to carry the war against the Saracens into the very heart of the Islamic world, namely, to the ports of the Hejaz and the Yemen, whence he hoped to penetrate to and sack the Holy Cities of Medina and Mecca themselves. No one but Renaud could have formed such a plan as this; but, before it could be realized, it was necessary for him firstly to retake Aqaba and then to acquire a fleet to transport his warriors to the coasts of Arabia. He proceeded, therefore, at Ascalon according to some of the Arab chroniclers, at Kerak according to others, to construct his ships in pieces, and then began lengthy negotiations with the Beduin of the desert for their transport by camel to the distant Gulf.

His courage and patience were rewarded. After a long and, it appears, costly journey, the component parts of the fleet reached the head of the Gulf, the Sea of Qulzum of the Saracens, and the galleys and smaller craft were duly assembled and manned. The fleet was divided into two squadrons, one of which concentrated on the siege of Graye and Ailat, while the other set out on its astounding filibustering expedition against the coasts of Araby. Although few of the details of this heroic adventure have been preserved to us, we know that throughout the second half of 1182 and the early part of 1183 the Crusading fleet remained master of and terrorized both shores of the Red Sea, carried the Cross into almost fabulous regions where it had never before been seen, and actually raided as far south as Aden. It intercepted, pillaged and burned pilgrim convoys proceeding to the Hejaz as well as merchantmen of the Yemen, and seized great quantities of food-stuffs destined for the victualling of Medina and Mecca. Caravans now feared to set out on the pilgrimage, while the inhabitants of the Holy Cities began to believe, in the words of a Moslem chronicler, that the Last Judgment had come.

The sad end of this expedition at the hands of the Egyptian Admiral Lulu, while the ships' companies of the second squadron were actually preparing to march inland to the capture of Medina, must not detain us here: suffice it to say that Renaud's effort was the high-water mark of the romance of Aqaba until in our own time Lawrence concluded one of the most dramatic chapters of his campaign as he "raced through a driving sandstorm down to Aqaba, four miles farther, and splashed into the sea on July the sixth, just two months after our setting out from Wejh."

Allusion has been made to Aqaba's Mamluk castle, the only architectural monument of its antiquity. It is to-day sufficiently well preserved to be the barracks of the Aqaba detachment of the Arab Legion, and inside it can still be read the inscription of its founder, the penultimate of the Mamluk Sultans of Egypt:

PLATE XV

AQABA.

King Husein's Shield.

The Castle.

[*To face p.* 228.

"Has been erected this blessed castle by order of our Lord His Most Excellent Majesty Abul Nasr Qansua al-Ghuri, Sultan of Islam and of the Faithful, Slayer of infidels and heretics and Reviver of justice in the world."

On the outer walls is a later inscription, recording the reconstruction of the castle in the year of the Hejra 996 (1588) by the Ottoman Sultan Murad III.

Over the entrance, flanked by two towers of the Mamluk period picturesque with alternate courses of pink and white stone, is a plastic reminder of one of the last acts in the long drama of Aqaba; it is incidentally one of the most recent contributions to Moslem heraldry. As the Latin kingdom of Jerusalem at its death-gasp retreated northwards to Acre, so in 1924 did King Husein, driven from the Hejaz by Ibn Saud, withdraw to the north, until at the end we find him keeping his transitory state in Aqaba with such resources as in its decay the little town could afford. A stone panel embellished with the representation of a fortress surrounded by an achievement of flags, guns and swords records the passage of the last of the Moslem kings who have held their Court in Aqaba, while close at hand is a small fountain with which he endowed the town, a gift typical of the forms of charity induced by the thirsty lands of Islam.

Aqaba has fallen from its high estate, but I believe that it has still the germs of life, that it has dropped to a nadir from which it can rise again. It is interesting that the only allusion to it in the Qoran has to do with the fish with which its Gulf is so well stocked, for the experiment is now being tried of sending regular consignments of fresh fish from Aqaba to Ma'an and thence by rail to Amman, where it seems that they can compete with supplies from the Mediterranean. And it is not impossible that with the farther economic development of Transjordan it may revive again in other respects, and that even its pilgrim-traffic might one day be to some extent resumed. In the meantime the "Vierkleur" of Transjordan—white for the Omayyads, black for the Abbasids, green for the Fatimites, red for the Hashimites—floats over its little white *sarai*, epitome of its history during the last twelve and a half centuries.

A RESTORATION NAVAL CHAPLAIN IN THE MEDITERRANEAN

X

A RESTORATION NAVAL CHAPLAIN IN THE MEDITERRANEAN

THE reign of Charles II was a period of great importance in the history of the English Navy. It was a period of rapid progress in size and efficiency, a period in which were laid the foundations of that British supremacy at sea which became an established fact in the wars with Napoleon. The Restoration Navy had the advantage of constant activity for, if there was peace with Holland or France, there were always the Barbary States to be kept in order or punished for their intolerable piracy and acts of aggression. Gibraltar was not yet British, but in the port of Tangier, which Charles had acquired as a part of his Queen's dowry and retained until 1683, England possessed a useful base for her activities in the Western Mediterranean. Tripoli, in particular, was a source of much trouble at this time; and in 1674 it became necessary to despatch an expedition under Admiral Sir John Narborough against this truculent corsair State. The operations against Tripoli continued during the early spring of 1675, and were crowned with success. The corsairs were compelled to sue for peace, and in March,

1675, Sir John imposed on them a treaty, which curbed very materially their power for mischief. Shortly afterwards, however, the people of Tripoli rose against the Government which had signed the treaty. The Dey, Ibrahim, barely escaped with his life, the treaty was ignored, and the pirates resumed their depredations on English shipping. Fortunately the Admiral was still in the Mediterranean. He reappeared before Tripoli with eight frigates and without farther parley proceeded to batter the city with such effect that the new Government promptly sued for a renewal of the peace.

Among the eye-witnesses of the later operations was an interesting but little known personage, a truly typical product of his time. This was the Reverend Henry Teonge, Chaplain of H.M.S. "Assistance," Captain William Houlding, a frigate which joined Sir John's flag off Tripoli in 1675. An old Cavalier, Teonge was Vicar of Spernall in Warwickshire, and was a man of fifty-four when *res angusta domi* drove him to leave his quiet country parish and to go to sea in the "Assistance." Happily for himself, his genial and sanguine temperament enabled him to bear with equanimity the effects of so sharp a transition. Human and humorous and a *bon viveur*, but well read, intelligent and with acute powers of observation, he contrived to extract a considerable measure of enjoyment and certainly much interest from his cruises, despite the dangers and discomforts which then attended a sea-faring career. Besides participating in the attack on Tripoli he visited,

as will be seen, a large number of countries bordering
on the Mediterranean, western and eastern, and
indulged in much good cheer; and he recorded his
experiences in his diary with quaint and pungent
humour and with the outspoken frankness of the age.
He died in 1690, in his seventieth year, and for more
than a century after his death the diary lay buried in
the library of a Warwickshire family until a discerning
London publisher bought it and printed it. In the
following pages I have made a selection from some of
the more interesting passages of the diary, allowing old
Teonge to speak for himself in his robust and graphic
language of his experiences on the Barbary Coast,
in Malta and in the Archipelago, Cyprus, Alexandretta, Aleppo and elsewhere in the outlying provinces
of the Grand Signor.

The diary begins with his departure from Spernall,
which was not unlike that of d'Artagnan from his home
in Gascony:

"*Thursday, May* 20, 1675. *Deus vortat bene!*

This day I began my voyage from my house at
Spernall, in the county of Warwick; with small
accouterments, saveing what I carried under me
in an olde sack. My steed like that of Hudibras,
for mettle, courage, and color (though not of the
same biggnes:) and for flesh, one of Pharaoh's
leane mares, ready to cease (for hunger) on those
that went before her, had shee not beene short
winged; or rather leaden heeled. My stock of

235

monys was also proportionable to the rest; being little more than what brought me to London, in an old coate, and britches of the same; an old payre of hose and shooes; and a lethern dublett of 9 yeares olde and upward. Indeeds (by reason of the suddennes of my jurny), I had nothing but what I was ashamed of; save only

An old fox broade-sword, and a good black gowne ;
And thus Old Henry cam to London towne.

Hither was I no sooner arived, but I was court-eously received; first by Leiuetenant Haughton, with bottells of claret, etc; and after, by Capt. William Houlding, with entertainment of the same fashon.

Thence to the Longe Reach; where I was that morning entred on board Chaplen to His Magesty in his Frigott Assistance, of 56 gunns, and under the command of Captain Will. Houlding; and returned againe that night to London.

And now a small sea-bed is my unum neces-sarium (though I wanted almost every thing else): a thing that I could not bee without; nor knew I how to compas it. I sent for som bedding into the country; and I try som friends to borrow som monys; but all in vaine; and all to retreeve my cloake, left longe since (in pawn), not at Troas (as Saint Paule's was), for his was recovered only with demaund; mine could not be got by fayer or foule meanes. Seeing no other meanes I rem'bred the poet:

ἀργυρίαις λόγχαισι μαχοῦ καὶ πάντα κράτησις.

I sum'on all my forces, and I borrow 5s. of my landlady; and thus I redeemed my cloake: lying only for 10s. Haveing done thus, my leane mare, with saddle, bridle, and bootes, and spurrs, I sold to my landlord for 26s., upon condition that if 26s. was sent to him in a fortnight's time, the mare might be redeemed, but the other things lost. And my cloake I pawne againe for 40s.

On the 1st June he embarked at Blackwall and, after a slow and uneventful passage down Channel (interrupted at various points for the pressing of seamen) and across the Bay of Biscay, the "Assistance" arrived off Lisbon on the 10th July.

"July 10.

Wee are past the Rock of Lysbon, but could not discover it by reason of the fogg. This day our noble Capt. feasted the officers of his small squadron with 4 dishes of meate, viz. 4 excellent henns and a peice of porke boyled, in a dish; a giggett of excellent mutton and turnips; a peice of beife of 8 ribbs, well seasoned and roasted; and a couple of very fatt greene geese; last of all, a greate Chesshyre cheese; a rare feast at shoare. His liquors were answerable; viz. Canary, Sherry, Renish, Clarett, white wine, syder, ale, beare, all of the best sort; and punch like [*i.e.*, as plentiful as] ditch water, with which wee conclude the day and weeke in drinking to the Kinge, and all that wee love; while the wind blows fayre.

Sunday, July 11.

The wind is very calme, and I preacht a sermon, text, Luke VIII., 15.

July 22.

This morne wee are neare the edge of the Gulfe of Lyons; a very dangerouse place for stormes; lying north from us as we sayle. The winde very fayre, and the sea quiet enough, though usually here about tis very ruff. This day wee have a fayre on our quarter deck; viz. our pursor opens his pack, and sells to the value of 30 pounds or more, shirts, drawers, wascots, neckcloats, stockings, shooes, and takes no mony for them; this is newes.

July 26.

This morn brings with it a pleasant gale after our yesterday's calm; and this morning (as tis the use at sea) is black Munday with the boyes, who are many of them whipt with a catt with 9 tayles for their misdemeanurs, by the boarsons mate.

August 1.

This morn wee com near Malta; or as twas called formerly Melitta, from the abundance of hony they have there, gathered by the bees from the annice seeds, and flowers thereof, which groe on this Iland abundantly. Before wee com to the cytty a boate with the Malteese flagg in it coms to us to know whence wee cam. Wee told them from England; they asked if wee had a bill of health for prattick, viz. entertaynment; our Capt. told them that he had no bill but what was in his gunns mouths. Wee came on and anchored in the harbour betweene the old towne and the new, about 9 of the clock; but must waite the governour's leasure to have leave to com on shoare; which was detarded, because our Capt. would not salute the cytty, except they would retaliate. At last cam the Consull with his attendants to our ship (but would not com on board till our Capt. had been on shoare) to tell us that wee had leave to com on shoare 6 or 8 or 10 at a time, and might have any thing that was there to be had; with a promise to accept our salute kindly. Whereupon our Capt. tooke a glasse of sack and drank a health to King Charles, and fyred 7 gunns: the cytty gave us 5 againe; which was more than they had don to all our men of warr that cam thither before. This being done our Capt. sent his lieuetenant and som more of our gentlemen to salute the Grand Master; and to tell him that he would waite on him the next morning. . . . The hospital is a vast structure, wherin their sick and woonded lye. Tis so broade that 12 men may with ease walke a brest up the midst of it; and the bedds are on each syd, standing on 4 yron pillars, with white curtens, and vallands, and covering, extremely neate, and kept cleane and sweete; the sick served all in sylver plate, and it containes above 200 bedds below, besyds many spatious roomes in other quadrangles with in, for the chiefe cavaliers and knights, with pleasant walkes and gardens; and a stately house for the chiefe doctor and other his attendants.

The Lazaretta (a place on purpose for such as

are sick of the plague or other pestilentiall diseases;
which in regard of the heate of that country doth
often rage there) lyes closse under their outermost wall, and is extremely neatly kept and
provided for.

This Cytty is compassed almost cleane round
with the sea, which makes severall safe harbours
for hundreds of shipps. The people are generally
extremely courteous, but especially to the English.
A man can not demonstrate all their excellencys
and ingenuitys. Let it suffice to say thus much of
this place: viz. Had a man no other buisnes to
invite him, yet it were sufficiently worth a man's
cost and paines to make a voyage out of England
on purpose to see that noble cytty of Malt, and
their works and fortifications about it. Severall of
their knights and cavaliers cam on board us, 6 at
on time, men of sufficient courage and friendly
carriage, wishing us good successe in our voyage;
with whom I had much discourse, I being the only
entertainer, because I could speake Latine; for
which I was highly esteemed, and much invited
on shoare again."

On the 9th August the "Assistance" reaches Tripoli,
where she finds the "Henrietta," flying Sir John Narborough's flag, and the frigates "Newcastle," "Dragon,"
"Swallow," "Dartmouth," "Roebuck" and "Mary
Rose."

"*August* 16.

This morn (as wee ly at anchor) 4 slaves ventered
to swim from the shoare to our shipps, to make their

PLATE XVI

The Hospital of the Knights, Malta.

The Grand Harbour, Malta, in the time of Teonge.

From a fresco in the Palace, Valletta.

[*To face p.* 240.

escapes; whereof on of them was overtaken by a Trypoly boate, and carryed back to be miserably tortured. The other 3 cam on board us; on of them almost dead, being taken up by the Admirall's boate: the other twoe were tooke up by our boate. On of them had got a peice of an olde raile, and a goate skinn, which he had tyed together at boath ends, and blowed it full of wind, and made it fast to the olde raile: with that engine they cam safe on board. Two of them were Greeks, and the other a French man.

September 8.

Now about seven of the clock two lusty shipps are coming out of the harbour of Trypoly in the sight of all our fleete. Every on makes ready to fight them; but immediately there fell a thick mist between them and us, that wee could not see them just when they cam out. They had also a fresh gale, and wee scarce so much wind as would stir a ship. Two of our ships that were crusing eastward did almost meete them, and on of them, viz: the Dartmouth, made som shott at them, but all in vaine, for they clearly out sayled us all; in so much, that by 3 of the clock they had run us all quite out of sight."

The escape of the two corsairs necessitated an alteration in the Admiral's plans. Fearing that English merchant shipping in the Mediterranean would thereby be endangered, he sent three of his ships, "Dragon," "Dartmouth" and "Assistance," in pursuit of the pirates. Their orders were to proceed together to the Archipelago and there part company, "Dragon" and "Dartmouth" making for Smyrna and "Assistance" for "Scanderoond" (Alexandretta).

"October 4.

This morning (haveing had a prosperous gale all night) wee are in sight of that famous iland of Cyprus, once in the possession of the English; and a very plentifull iland, stored with good things.

October 14.

And here we ly, becalmed all this while, and very hott; and now wee tow in our ship, for wee can gett her in no other way. And at 4 in the afternoone wee com to an anchor in Scanderoond Roade; where wee find 3 ships at anchor. The Syppio, whoe saluts us with 5 gunns, wee returne 3; she thanks us with on more. The William and Thomas gave us 3 gunns; we answered with on. The 3d was a Venetian, and gave us 7 gunns; and wee returned 5. Then went out Leiuetenant and Pursor on shoare, to see what provision or liquor was to be gott. The Consull, Mr. Low, cam on board to welcom us, and brought foules and herbs to us. At his going off wee gave him 5 gunns, and our trumpetts sounding—Mayds, where are your harts, etc.

October 22.

No thing done but goeing too and froe to shoare and from shoare. But on Wensday last fell much raine, with thunder and lightening; and wee all saw severall spouts, boath drawn up from the sea, and also faull in to the sea againe. But especially wee saw on great spout drawne up out of the bay, and carryd to land; and wee saw it breake and fall on the syd. It fell neare the house of a servant to the Caddee, and drive it downe, and also carrye it and all in it away, with him selfe, his wife, and 2 children. The woman was this day found at Asshen Poynt (not above a leage from us), beaten all in peices.

November 3.

Wee scrape our quarter deck, mend sayles, and fetch butts from shoare. At 5 a clock cam the Greate Basshaw from the Grand Senior, and many more brave Turks with him to see our ship: we entertaynd him with our trumpetts and 7 gunns, and 7 at his going. He goes his syrkett every yeare in the nature of on of our judges, to heare grievances, and to doe justice, and to enquire into the state of all affayres in this syrkett, once a yeare. And so the greate Turke sends of these men every yeare through out all his teritorys. This Bashaw hath 500 horse attending on him, and goes in greate state, and is as it were in the nature of an English Collonell, but that he hath also the power of lyfe and death at his owne pleasure.

November 8.

I began to nett my sylke gyrdle.

November 9.

I was invited to dinnar with our Captaine, and our Doctor, our Pursor, Capt. Mauris, and Capt. North, to our Consulls on shoare; where wee had a princelike dinnar; and every health that wee dranke, every man broake the glasse he drank in; so that before night wee had destroyd a whole chest of pure Venice glasses; and when dinner was ended, the Consull presented every on of us with a bunch of beads, and a handfull of crosse, for which he sent to Jherusalem on purpose, as he tolde us afterwards.

December 6.

This part of Asya is called Cylicia. And in this very place (which is called the Straits of Cylicia, which lys betweene Tarsus and Scanderoond, and is the greate roade way betweene Constantinople and Jherusalem; and is a very narrow passage betweene the sea and the mountaine Taurus) did Alexander the greate in person, with 30,000 men, give Darius a greate overthroe, who had at least an hundred thousand men. And in memory of this his victory, he built a small cytty, and called it Alexandria; and to distinguish it from Alexandria in Egypt, it was called Alexandretta, and now Scanderoond. The bay is rather an elbow than a half-moone; and the towne stands in the southeast corner, which hath beene far biger. There remayns also the ruins of an old brick castle, but it could never be of any considerable strength. But on of the Gaws of Scanderoond began the

244

platforms of a stronge fortification, and built it 6 or 10 yards high, and the greate gate leading into it was built quite over the arch; but the Grand Seniore haveing notice of it, and knowing not but that it might prove a nursery of rebellion (for the Turks are very jealous people), sent 2 mutes, which brought away his heade, and so the work lyes as he left it to this very day.

The headsman that was sent for this Gaw's head, had command to bring 4 other Gaws' heads also, which order he executed; but going over the plaines of Antioch, he had accidentally lost on of them: he knowing not what course to take (knowinge also that his owne head must goe for that which he had carelessly lost) did in his jurny lite of a poore Arabian, who had a lawdible black beard; the headsman maks no more a doe, but strangles the man, and takes of the skine of his head and face, and stuffs it with cotton (which is their way of beheading, and they doe it so artifically that the very countenance and complexion of the man remaineth firme), and brought it amonge the rest, and it passed currant. The headsman himselfe tolde mee this sam story at Aleppo.

Here is an art (I meane from the 3 factorys) to send a pigion single, and somtimes 2 together, from hence to Aleppo upon any sudden occasion of shipping coming in, or any other buisnes. The pigions are bread at Aleppo, and brought downe on horseback in cages, and when occasion serves, a small note made fast to their wing, closse to theyr body with a sylke, yet so as not to hurt the

wing; and then take them to the topp of the factory, and let him goe, and the pigion will fly home
(which any of our pigions would also doe), and the
pigion coming home, thinking to creepe in to his
old habitation, is caught as it were in a cofer trapt,
and taken, and examined."

"Assistance," having failed to find the corsairs, now
prepares to rejoin the fleet, with two English merchantmen in convoy. Off Zante she falls in with "Dartmouth" and "Dragon" convoying four merchantmen.

> "*December* 25.
>
> Christman day wee keepe thus. At 4 in the
> morning our trumpeters all doe flatt their trum-
> petts, and begin at our Captain's cabin, and thence
> to all the officers' and gentlemen's cabins; playing
> a levite at each cabin doore, and bidding good
> morrow, wishing a merry Christmas. After they
> goe to their station, viz. on the poope, and sound
> 3 levitts in honour of the morning. At 10 wee goe
> to prayers and sermon; text, Zacc. IX., 9. Our
> Captaine had all his officers and gentlemen to
> dinner with him where we had excellent good
> fayre: a ribb of beife, plume-puddings, minct pyes,
> etc; and plenty of good wines of severall sorts;
> dranke healths to the King, to our wives and
> friends; and ended the day with much civill myrth.

> *January* 6, 1676.
>
> Very ruff weather all the last night, and all this
> day. Wee are now past Zante: had wee beene there
> this day, wee had seene a greate solemnity; for this

day being 12 Day, the Greeke Bishop of Zante
doth (as they call it) baptise the sea, with a greate
deale of ceremony; sprinkling their gallys and
fishing-tackle with holy-water. But wee had much
myrth on board, for we had a greate kake made,
in which was put a beane for the king, a pease for
the queen, a cloave for the knave, a forked stick
for the coockold, a ragg for the slutt. The kake
was cutt into severall peices in the great cabin, and
all put into a napkin, out of which every on took
his peice, as out of a lottery, then each peice is
broken to see what was in it, which caused much
laughter, to see our leiuetenant prove the coockold,
and more to see us tumble on over the other in the
cabin, by reason of the ruff weather.

January 15.

This morning wee warp out of the harbour,
with 6 merchantmen and a doggar, which wee are
to convoy towards the Straits mouth. Here also
wee took in 2 months provision, and fresh water.
And as wee goe out, wee meete 6 gallys of Malta,
coming in in all their pompe, and they salute us,
and wee them, and part. And heare at Malta (which
was very strainge to mee) at this time of the yeare
wee bought radishes, cabbidges, and excellent colly
flowers, and large ons for 1d. a peice.

January 30.

By 8 wee are at anchor in the harbour at Malta;
where the Ginny and the Martin salute us with 5
gunns a peice; wee answer with 3 to each. Here wee
are tolde of the joyfull news of Sir John's burning

of 4 Trypoly men of warr in their owne harbour;
and how wee tooke their guard boat first, and killed
all that were in her, and so went in, and fyred the
ships, and cam out again with out any man being
hurt. No sermon to day, our Captaine not being
well. The plague is in the cytty, so that we have
no prattick.

This day being the day of our King's marter-
dome, wee show all the signes of morning as
possible wee can, viz. our jacks and flaggs only
half staffe high; and at 5 a clock in the afternoone
our ship fyred 20 gunns; the trumpetts at the close
ringing the bells on the trumpetts very dolefully,
and also the gunns fyreing at halfe a minute distance. Then the Dartmouth fyre 18 gunns at the
same distance, and their trumpetts also the same;
and our 2 merchants fyred 16 a peice. After all our
trumpetts sounded Well-a-day, the Dartmouth did
the same, and so were ended the day mornfully;
which made the Maltees much woonder, till they
understood the reason of it.

February 4.

This day dined with us Sir Roger Strickland,
Captaine Temple, Captaine Harrice, and on gentleman more. Wee had a gallant baked pudding, an
excellent legg of porke and colliflowers, an excellent dish made of piggs' pettitoes, 2 rosted piggs,
one turkey cock, a rosted hogg's head, 3 ducks, a
dish of Cyprus burds and Pistachees and dates
together, and store of good wines.

February 5.

God bless those that are at sea! The weather is very bad.

February 6.

Bad weather still. No sermon to day; the Captaine not well.

February 7.

I dined on board the Ginny; and had harty welcom.

February 15.

The Grand Master cam to visit our Admirall, whoe gave him 11 gunns.

February 16.

I bought a wigg of Mr. Selby for 3 dollars, and som Syracosa wine; and a hatt cost 3 dollars.

February 22.

This day we saw a greate deale of solemnity at the launching of a new bryganteene of 23 oares, built on the shoare very neare the water. They hoysted 3 flaggs in her yesterday, and this day by 12 they had turned her head neare the water; when as a greate multitude of people gathered together, with severall of their knights and men of quality, and a clowd of fryars and churchmen. They were at least 2 howers in their benedictions, in the nature of hymns or anthems, and other their ceremonys; their trumpetts and other musick playing often. At last 2 friars and an attendant went in to her, and kneeling downe prayd halfe an howre, and layd their hands on every mast and other places of the vessell, and sprinkled her all over with holy water. Then they cam out and hoysted a pendent, to signify shee was a man of warr; and then at once thrust her into the water, where shee no sooner was, but they fyred 21 chambers, and rowed to our Admirall and gave him a gunn, whoe gave them another. Then she went into the cove where all their gallys lye, and was welcomed with abundance of gunns. And there are 4 more just ready to be launched, all for the coasts of Tripoly.

February 24.

The Portchmouth cam out last night. Wee stand for Trypoly, 14 brave shipps, and stand almost in a line.

February 25.

By 10 this morning, by a pendent on the mizon peake, our Admirall calls on the captaines to a consultation; for wee had before seene the eastern coasts of Trypoly.

With in an hower each of them was on board againe. But the wind rose this afternoone on a sudden, and hindred our designe.

March 4.

This morning wee are all close before Trypoly, and I suppose this will be joyfull Satterday to them; for boath the King and Queene of Tunis have beene at Trypoly since wee burnt their ships; and are to goe to the Greate Turke for ayd against those that have driven them from thence. They have desyred a convoy from our Admirall, and will make a peace betweene us and Trypoly. His name is Hopsiby, and tis related that he hath 700 concubines.

At on a clock cam a halfe-gally to our Admirall, and saluted him with all her gunns; our Admirall thanked him with 11, and then let fly all his pendents. At 5 a clock boath the bryganteene and the half-gally sent offe, and our Admirall gave them 11 gunns; and the halfe gally gave all shee had; but still our Admirall did out doe them in civility. The Bristow gave them 9, and the Portchmouth 9, as they went by them.

With in the harbour the King of Tunnis his ship saluted them with 8 gunns, and the shoare saluted them with 10, as I counted them; but the peace is not yet fully concluded.

No prayers to day by reason of buisnes. The peace, as it is sayd, is concluded; the King of Tunis being the only agent in it. The Trypolees are to give us 80,000 peices of eight, and to release all the slaves that belonge to the crowne of England, and to release 4 merchants of Lygorne, and a knight of Malta; yet these must pay a certaine summ of monys; and this did bite sore, for betweene the Maltees and the Turks this is their absolute law, that whosoever of them is taken in actuall armes is never to be ransumed.

Tis the most honourable peace that ever yet was

251

made with the Turks. They were very loath to pay any monys, but were so affrited at our bold attempt to burninge their ships, and also as much to see our fyre-shipps there, that they were forced to graunte what our Admirall would have.

March 8.

The articles are now all signed on boath syds; and the Trypolees sent off the articles, and at 5 in the morning fyred all the gunns about their cytty twice over, which was answered by all our fleete, and the peace is absolutely ratifyd.

At 8 a clock our ship takes leave of Sir John, and salutes him with 11 gunns and 3 cheares; and he nobly salutes us with as many; we return him thanks with 5, and so part; and our ship with the Dartmouth and 3 merchant ships stand for Scanderoond. This day I began to make buttons for som new cloaths.

March 29.

Wee discover the west end of Cyprus, but far off. Since yesterday 12 a clock to 6 this evening wee have runn 200 miles.

March 30.

The wind is so crosse that wee can not com to the anchoring place.

March 31.

At 8 wee com to an anchor in the bay of Saline; and are saluted by our merchants with 7, 5-5 gunns.

About 10 I went a shoare, the sea being very ruff. The fort, standing neare the water, and faceing the roade, is very inconsiderable; haveing not above 9 pittifull gunns in it. Uppon the Mareene stands a small towne, consisting of coffee-houses, and shopps, and ware-houses, and other places where wine is to be sould. In the middle of the streete lay severall hundredds of hogg-skins full of wines, which at first sight I tooke for so many singed hoggs. . . . West from this, about a little mile, stands Larneca; a pleasant walke leading to it; and is of itselfe a pleasant village, beautifyd with severall handsom structures, such as that country affords; where wee had good entertainment, and excellent muskadell at our Consull's house. The feilds have little grasse therabout, but are overgrowne with camamile, marigolds, muscovy, etc. And great store of caper bushes, palm trees, almond trees, and olives; and such plenty of tyme, and so bigg growne, that the people stock it up to burne, as wee doe furse or ghosse.

Excellent wines, white and red, which they make in the mountaine, and bring it downe in hogg-skins, like little ferkins.

Sunday, April 9.

Wee are entred into the great bay that leads to Scanderoond. The buisnes of our ship hinders our devotions.

April 17.

A very blustering day. And this is (as it is called by our sea men) the last day of Lent; that is, the day wheren the last boyling of the beife that was bought at Cyprus, was flung over board; for the meate was so bad, that they chose rather to eate bread dry, then to eate that meate. That was much to our Purser's discreditt.

April 29.

This day about 10 of the clock, Captaine Harman of the Gynny and my selfe, and a Janizary, and his man, and my man, doe begin our jurny towards Aleppo. At a place calld Byland, about 10 miles from Scanderoond wee dine, at an olde Greek's house, with good mutton steaks; and drank good wine, and payd a dollar. . . . The Captaine and I have a tent pitched over us; an old Turkey carpet spread under, and a rowle of matting layd to lay our heads on. But what with the fleas and lyce that were in that carpett, and the froggs that were croakeing all about us, as also the hooteing of the jack-calls, I could not sleepe on winke, but we sat up and drank wine and brandee, of which wee brought good store with us; and there I did eat polloe with the Turke.

Sunday, April 30.

Haveing rod a longe way in this plaine (*sc.* of Antioch) we com at the last to a small village, the worst that ever I saw; the houses being of nothing but reedes, and peices of the barke of trees covering the tops of them in the nature of hollow tyles. Tis inhabited by Arabeans, whoe have abundance of these buffeloes, and som few cowes, hoggs, som sheepe, and abundance of henns. Heare very neare to the houses are abundance of buffeloe calves, every on of them tyd (like so many beares) to a stake, where I suppose they give them milke. The people were many of them milking these cattell when the Captaine, and I, and our Janizary cam thither; for our Janizary had a friend lay there, which he was to call on, and he brought us out of the way to that place. And many foule women were makeing of butter of the buffeloes milke, which they put into calf's skin, or hogg's skin, and so doe rowle it, and kneade it on the ground till it be a substance, more like greace then butter boath for looks and taste; for the cheife lady of the towne (as I suppose by her habite) presented us with som of it, and a little of that would goe farr."

On the 1st May Teonge and his companions reached Aleppo, then a place of far greater commercial importance than it is to-day. It was at that time one of the principal marts on the trade route between East and West; and England, France and Holland maintained there factories of their respective Levant Companies. During the seventeenth and eighteenth centuries the English factory of Aleppo was in a highly flourishing condition. Its head performed at the same time the functions of English Consul, and the members lived a collegiate life in the factory building, ruled in civil and commercial matters by the Consul, in spiritual affairs by their Chaplain.

"*May* 1.

Where as soon as wee com to the enterance into

255

the towne, Captaine Harman and myselfe were placed in the front, the 2 Janizarys only goeing before us; and all the rest of the gentlemen (of which at least 40 cam to meete us) cam a loofe off behind us, as is the custom there, to signify that wee were straingers. The people boath men and woemen cam out to gaze after us, whilst he and I rodd on together very merily. All the Franks accompany us to the factory; where first the Consull himselfe, and then all the rest of the gentry there present, takes us by the hand, and bids us wellcom. Here the Captaine leaves me, and goes to another English house. Then the Consull, Mr. Gamaliell Nightingall, takes me by the hand, and leads me through a longe hall, into his chamber; to which place cam all the rest of the Franks in particular, that had not done it before, to bid mee welcom to the towne. After a while the Consull takes mee by the hand, and leades me 'thwart a stately roome, which is their chappell, and puts me into a very fayre chamber, and bids mee call it my home, etc.

May 6.

This morning early (as it is the custom all summer longe) at the least 40 of the English, with his worship the Consull, rod out of the cytty about 4 miles to the Greene Platt, a fine vally by a river syde, to recreate them selves. There a princely tent was pitched; and wee had severall pastimes and sports, as duck-hunting, fishing, shooting, hand-ball, krickett, scrofilo; and then a noble dinner brought thither, with greate plenty of all sorts of wines, punch, and lemonads; and at 6 wee returne all home in good order, but soundly tyred and weary.

May 13.

This day I went with 4 more gentlemen to see som of the great houses in the cytty; for it is not permitted to any stranger to com into the castle, except he intend not to com out againe.

The first wee went to was a Turk's house, viz. the Mussilem. He himselfe was not at home; but gone the day before to Stambole, alias Constantinople; but wee were kindly entertayned by a servant with tobacco and coffee, and were shewed severall very stately roomes. 'Twas a palace fitt for a King.

The 2d house wee visitted was a Jew's house; whear wee first knocked at the outermost gate, and a servant coming, wee told him our desyre was only to see the house; and he went in to acquaint his Master. Wee would not follow him in, because it was the Jew's sabbaoth day, and about two of the clock. On of the gentlemen of the house cam out himselfe, and led us in, and seemed to take it ill that wee would make any scruple at all of coming in; for, says he, I am much beholden to any stranger that he will take so much paines as to com to see my house. He led us into a spacious roome, in the midst of which was a large fountaine, with 4 cocks flinging up water, and falling into the fountaine; which was a square about 8 yards in compas. And each end of the roome was also a 4 square: and ascended 3 or 4 stepps; the square being spread over with rich carpetts, and velvett and plush longe cushens, richly embroydred with golde, lay closse on to another round about the carpetts. There were 4 gentlemen whoe were all three parts fuddled, and had been merry-makeing with their women, whoe had absented themselves at our approaching (but som of them peeped at us at a dore as wee cam by them). For thus they spend their sabaoth; in the about sunriseing they doe their devotions, and all the day following they spend in frollikeing with their women. They made us extreamly welcom with exceeding good wines of severall sorts, and severall sorts of biskott kakes and sweet-meats, such as I never saw before; and shewed us their gardens, and tame pigions, and every thing but their women. This whole streete is all inhabited by Jewes, where wee mett boys and gyrles as fayre and as well complexioned as English.

The third house was also a Turk's house, and a greate man; viz. the Gaw, or Master of the Janizarys. Here wee were also courteously enter-tayned with tobacco and coffee, and cocolate; and here wee saw som of his breeding mares, which were valued at a high rate; but lookt like very jades. Thence wee cam back to dinner, only just looking into another house as we cam."

The party were now about to rejoin their ships at Alexandretta, but on the 15th May received word from the Turkish authorities that they were not to leave the city.

"*May* 16.

A little after ten a clock, our noble Consull, attended with most of the English in towne, went to the Caddee (who is in the nature of a Ld. Cheife Justice) to know the cause of our restraint. There was a greate chayre richly gilt, carryd by 2 men before the Consull all along the streete; and when we cam to his house the chayre was carryd up into the roome, and placed just against the Caddee, who sate like a tayler on his carpetts, with a boy leaneing on a pillow closse by him on his right hand, and 2 more with him like Counsellors. The Caddee had on his head instead of his turbate, a globe, neatly covered with fine linnen, which lay all in very neate pleats, very exactly done, and was neare of the compas of a strike or bushell. Our Consull presently sate downe in his chayre, with his hatt on, and cockt; and haveing dranke a cup of cocolate, and had his beard perfumed (as is their custom, in token of his honour), he propounds our case very breifly, but by an interpreter. The Caddee by his interpreter gives his answer, and pleades ignorance in the buisnes. But in coms an old Turke, in poore cloathes, stroaking his longe beard a wry, with his nether lipp and chin quivering, holding out his left arme at its full length, with the 3 foremost fingers stretched out, and his thumb and little finger cluncht together in the middle of his hand; and pulling one of the little buttons that were on the bosum of his delaman, with the fore-finger and the thumb of his right hand (all of which are signs of verity of speech); and alleages that a Maltee cursare had taken a syke [*sc.* caique], which was laden with his goods, and that the English were accessary to it, and had bought many of his goods; and he proferd to make oath of this, though it was a very lye. After a little examination, his oath would not be taken; and the Caddee told us that wee might goe when wee pleased. Notwithstanding all this, at on a clock a messenger was sent to deny Captaine Harman's passage.

May 19.

This morning our Consull being allmost impatient, knowing that our shipps were ready to sayle for England, being accompanyed with a greate traine of brave English men, and also som Dutch and French, went bouldly to theire Seraglio, a very gallant place; where wee find the Caddee, the Meane, the Mussilem, and the Master of the Janizarys (the 4 governors of the cytty) all together. After the ceremonys before specifyd were over, our Consull began with greate courage to charge them with breach of articles, and to demand satisfaction for our false imprisonment; and told them that if he could not be heard there, he would goe with lights to Stambole, and make the Greate Turke acquainted with the buisnes. This dispute grew higher and higher for at least halfe an hower; the old Turke aggravating what he had alleged, with a greate deale of earnestnes and confidence;

I might say, impudence. In the heate of all this discourse cam in a packett from Stamboule to our Consull, which he commaunded to be opened before them all; for, says hee, there may be in it somthing may concerne our busines: and so it proved; for there was an order or expresse to the Mussellem from the Grand Seniour, to confirm and establish all the commands and priviledges that were formerly made concerning the English. At the sight of which, the Turks lookt very dijectedly on upon the other, and presently gave us all our liberty without paying so much as an asper: the Musellem speakeing these words in their language, "The order is good, and must be observed by my head;" makeing all of them a low bow to us all.

So back wee returne with greate tryumph and rejoycing; and all provide for our jurny next morning. But such a parting of friends did I never see. The kind treate, and loath to depart, ended at my chamber; for the Consull went to each of their chambers particularly to bid them farewell, and mine was the last he visitted, being the next to his owne, where he gave me 2 chekeens [sequins]."

On the 20th May Teonge and his companions, accompanied by several gentlemen of the factory, whom he calls "Alopeenes," leave Aleppo, and reach Alexandretta two days later. On the 25th the squadron sets sail.

"*May* 29.

The Byrth Day and Restoration Day of our soveraine King Charles II. I preacht a sermon:

text Psal. CXVIII., 24. After dinner our Captaine began the King's health, and fyred 11 gunns; the Providence 9; the Martin 7: the Alopeenes give us wines galloore. And much about sunn setting wee see som part of the iland of Cyprus.

June 5.

I goe on shoare to buy wine to carry (God willing) into England; and I dined at our Consull's at Larneca."

During June and July the "Assistance" is much becalmed, not making Malta until the 23rd July.

"July 25.

At 10 this morning wee are under sayle and, God willing, for fayre England. Boone voyagio! our ship is very leaky.

August 10th.

Wee are closse under Monte Christo, a high rock in the sea; and suddenly wee have Illbay or Lillbow on our starboard syde, and have another flatt iland on our larboard, called Planosa. This day our noble Alopeenes did make grande festo for all the gentlemen in our squadron, where wee had a noble Venetian belonging to the Thomas and Francis, whoe brought with him from Smyrna a Greeke lady, at a vast charge to him; and made us happy with her company at our ship at dinner. Shee was woondrous rich in habite, and counted the beauty of the Levant, but I have seene far handsomer in England amonge our milk mayds. Tis calme all this night."

Not so, however, during the rest of the voyage. After rounding Gibraltar, the luckless "Assistance" runs into dirty weather, and only with difficulty reaches England.

"*September* 14.

Stormy weather, and raine; a sad tempestuous night. A dangerous leaky shipp. And as bad, or worse, today.

Sunday, September 17.

About 4 in the morning the seas groe far more outragious, and breake clearly over our quarter deck; drive our hen-cubbs [coops] overboard; and washed on of our seamen cleane off the crotchett-yard. A second sea cam, and threw downe all our boomes; brake boath pinnace, and longe boate, on the decks, A third cam, and flung our anchor off the ship syd, flung the bell out of his place, brake off the carving, and pulld 2 planks a sunder in the midst of the ship, betweene decks, and just against the pump. Our forecastle was broake all downe longe before. Now the men are all dishartened, and expect nothing but the losse of ship and life. Our larboard gunnhill all broake up, a whole planke almost out betweene decks; men swimming about in the wast of the ship; and greate seas often breaking over us. I never saw such a Sunday, and I hope shall never forget to give God thanks for this day's deliverance; for it was a miracle that ever wee escaped. At last our Captaine and the rest, consulting, made a shift to put up a small fore-sayle, and put the ship before the wind. Many greate seas breake over us all this night, and we have little hopes of any safety yet.

September 18.

As bad still, and wee are glad wee can put our ship before the wind to com to any port; but wee strive for Lysbon in Portugall. God send us safe in any port! for our ship is miserably shaken, and our men all tyred off their leggs and much dishartened.

October 26.

I went a shoare to Famouth; and cam not away till Saturday 28. Here wee spent all my Turkish gold, viz. 4 good chekeens.

October 30.

A fayre day, but very cold.

October 31.

And so to day. On Arrowsmyth, for lying a shoare without leave, was ducked at the yard arms.

November 17.

Friday, the 17th of November, wee are payd off at Dedford; where wee leave the rottenest frigot that ever cam to England."

APPENDIX

(A) *Princes of Monaco.*

	Reigned.
Honoré II	1604–1662
Louis I	1662–1701
Anthony I	1701–1731
Louise Hippolyte	Feb.–Dec. 1731
James I	1731–1733
Honoré III	1733–1793 (dep.)
Honoré IV	1814–1819
Honoré V	1819–1841
Florestan I	1841–1856
Charles III	1856–1889
Albert I	1889–1922
Louis II	1922–

(B) *Reigning Princes of Liechtenstein.*

John Adam	1699–1712
Joseph Wenzel	1712–1718
Anthony Florian	1718–1721
Joseph John	1721–1732
John Charles	1732–1748
Joseph Wenzel (again) . . .	1748–1772
Francis Joseph	1772–1781
Aloysius I	1781–1805
John I	1805–1836
Aloysius II	1836–1858
John II	1858–1929
Francis I	1929–

(C) *Kings and Princes of Yvetot from* 1532.

Martin II, du Bellay (*jure uxoris* Isabeau Chenu)	1532–1559
Isabeau (*suo jure*)	1559–1589
René du Bellay	1589–1606
Martin III du Bellay . . .	1606–1637
Charles du Bellay	1637–1661
Claud de Crevant	1663–1676
Marie Louise ⎱ de Crevant Françoise Julie ⎰ . .	1676–1685
Françoise Julie (alone) . . .	1685–1688
Camillus I d'Albon	1688–1729
Claud d'Albon	1729–1749
Camillus II d'Albon . . .	1749–1772
Camillus III d'Albon . . .	1772–1789

266

(D) *Grand Dukes and Duchesses of Luxemburg.*

William I ⎱ Also Kings of the	. .	1815–1840
William II ⎰ Netherlands	. .	1840–1849
William III	. .	1849–1890
Adolphus	. . . . .	1890–1905
William IV	. . . . .	1905–1912
Mary Adelaide	. . . .	1912–1919
Charlotte	. . . . .	1919–

(E) *Rulers of Montenegro of the dynasty of Petrović.*

Danilo I ⎫	. . . . .	1697–1735
Sava ⎬ Vladikas	. . .	1735–1781
S. Peter I ⎭	. . .	1781–1830
Peter II	. . . . .	1832–1851
Danilo II, Prince	. . . .	1851–1860
Nicholas I, Prince, later King (*de jure* from 1918)	. . . . . .	1860–1921

(F) *Great Counts of the Republic of Poljica from the middle of the eighteenth century.*

Marcus Barič	. . . . .	1747–1760
George Novakovič	. . . .	1760–1768
Iovan Gerončić	. . . .	1768–1771
Francis Pavič	. . . . .	1771–1777
Iovan Gerončić	. . . .	1778
Andreas Barič	. . . .	1778–1783
George Novakovič	. . . .	1783–1789
Iovan Sičič	. . . . .	1789–1793
Matthaeus Kružičevic	. . .	1793–1796
Francis Pavič	. . . . .	1796
Francis Gojselič	. . . .	1796–1797
Marcus Zuljevič	. . . .	1797–1799
Matthaeus Mianovic	. . .	1799–1803
Iovan Čovič	. . . . .	1803–1807

INDEX

INDEX

Gotha, Almanach de, 36, 68
Grimaldi, dynasty of, 65–74, 265

Harden-Hickey, J. A. ("James I, Prince of Trinidad"), 28–9
Hauser, Kaspar, 122–30
Hejaz Railway, 222–3
Henry IV, King of England, 215–17
Henry IV, King of France, 60
Herbert, Aubrey, 160
Herzegovina, 169, 174–5
Hoffmannsthal, Hugo von, 144–5
Holy Roman Empire, the, 43, 106, 132, 134, 141–2
Honoré II, Prince of Monaco, 65–6, 71
Honoré III, Prince of Monaco, 67, 69, 72, 113 *n.*
Honoré IV, Prince of Monaco, 67, 70
Honoré V, Prince of Monaco, 67–8
Husein, King of the Hejaz, 229

Ibn Saud, 226, 229
Il-Khans, dynasty of the, 200–1
India, soldiers of fortune in, 17–18
Ingoldsby Legends, 139
Ionian Islands, Septinsular Republic of the, 176–7
Islam in Albania, 155
Ismail Kemal Bey, Albanian statesman, 152–3
Istria, 187–8, 193
Italy, 45, 48–9, 53, 103, 143, 187

Jedermann at Salzburg, 144–8
Jenghiz Khan, 200
Jerusalem, Order of S. John of, 81–2, 251
John the Blind, King of Bohemia, 106–8, 116
John II, Prince of Liechtenstein, 76–8, 113 *n.*
Josephine, Empress, 67, 122

Kanina, Albanian village of, 153
Karlsruhe, 121–2
Khizmeh, plain of, 223
Klek, 174
Korcha (Koritza), 152, 159
Kossovo Polje, battle of, 167

Lágosta, 153, 189
Lateran Treaty, 79
Latin menu at Salona, 181
Lawrence T. E. (T. E. Shaw), 223–4, 228
Lebaudy, Jacques, "Emperor of the Sahara," 32–6
Leo XII, Pope, 56
Liechtenstein, Principality of, 44, 45, 75–9, 103, 265
Lobster and locust, joint derivation of, 189
Long reigns in European history, 77, 113
Louis the Debonair, 57–9, 103
Louis XI, King of France, 22
Louis II, Prince of Monaco, 66, 72–3

Louis, "King of Transcaucasia-Vitan-vali," 37–40
Lovčen, Mt., 165, 167
Lusignan, dynasty of, 36–7, 207
Lussin, 187
Luxemburg, Grand Duchy of, 103–18, 266

"Maikop, Grand Duchess of," 38–40
Malta, 81, 117, 235, 238–40, 247–50, 262
Mamluks, the, 201, 225, 228–9
Manuel II Palæologus, Byzantine Emperor, 212–17
Maraschino of Zara, 187
Marinus, S., 45, 47
Martin II, last King of Yvetot, 93–4
Marmont, Marshal, Duke of Ragusa, 174, 177, 186
Mary Adelaide, Grand Duchess of Luxemburg, 114–15
Mayrena, C. M. de, "King of the Sedangs," 30–32
"Meistertrunk," Rothenburg play of the, 135
Melusine, the mermaid, 37
Meštrović, 178
Monaco, Principality of, 44, 65–74, 103
Mongols, the, 199–207, 217
Montenegro, 159, 160–7
Moresnet, 82–3
Mudawwara, 223–4

Napoleon I, Emperor, 48–9, 62, 67–8, 72, 87–8, 110, 122, 126, 131, 157, 176, 183
Napoleon III, Emperor, 49, 111
Narborough, Admiral Sir John, 233–4, 240–41, 250–52
Nassau, Family of, 110, 112–14
Nestorians, 201–4
Netherlands, Kingdom of the, 82, 110–12
Nicholas I, King of Montenegro, 113 *n.*, 157, 161, 163, 166
Noli, Mgr. Fan, 158
Nördlingen, 132, 134–6
Nuremberg, 122–8

Oberammergau, 122
Obrenović, King Alexander, 157
Oettingen, Princes of, 134
Oligarchies of the Adriatic, 177–8, 185
Ophir, 226
Orange-Nassau, House of, 110, 112–13
Oultre-Jourdain, Principality of, 226–7

Papal States, 48, 79–81
Pérasto, 168–9
Peter I, King of Cyprus, 36, 207–12
Peter I, King of Yugoslavia, 178
S. Peter I, Vladika of Montenegro, 164–5
Peter II, Vladika of Montenegro, 161, 165–6
Petrovič, dynasty of, 161–6, 266

269

INDEX

Picard, Henry, Mayor of London, banquet of, to five kings, 210-11
Pius VI, Pope, and Yvetot, 98
Pius VIII, Pope, 56
Pius IX, Pope, 49, 157
Pius XI, Pope, 81
Poljica, Great Counts of, 184-7, 266
Poljica, Republic of, 180, 182-7

Qoran, the, 230
Quarnerolo, the, 188
Qulzum, Sea of (Gulf of Aqaba), 227

Ragusa, 165, 169-78, 189
Ragusa, Rectors of, 177-8
Reinhardt, Herr, and the Salzburg Festival, 144-7
Restoration Navy, the, 233-4
Rimini, 45, 47, 54
Rjeka, 160-61
Roman Republic of 1849, the, 49
Rothenburg, 132-6
Russian refugees in Ragusa, 178

Safaitic inscriptions in the Khizmeh, 223-4
Sahara, "Empire" of the, 32-6
Salona, 179-81
Salzburg, 139-48
Salzburg Festival, 144-8
Salzburg, Prince-Bishops of, 139-42
Sand, George, 56-7, 64
San Marino, Republic of, 44-57, 103, 176
Sáseno, 153, 188-9
Scutari (Albania), 159-60
Scutari, Lake of, 160-61
Sedangs, "Kingdom" of the, 30-32
Sinai, 221-2
Skanderbeg, 158
Spain, 61-3, 66, 89, 109, 116
Spálato, 180-84
Stanhope, fourth Earl, 128-30
Sutorina, valley of the, 169, 174
Swan, Order of the, 131-2

Talleyrand, C. M. de, Duke of Benevento, 56, 67
Teonge, Rev. Henry, 234-64
Thirty Years' War, 134-6, 142
Tirana, 152, 154-6, 159
Tounens, Orllie Antony de, "King" of Araucania, 19-24
"Transcaucasia-Vitanvali, Kingdom of," 37-40
Transjordan, 223, 230
Traù, 181-2

Trinidad, "Principality" of, 28-9
Tripoli (Barbary), 233-4, 240-41, 250-52
Tryphon, S., Guild of, 168
Tsetinje, 154, 161-7
Turks, 159-60, 165, 174, 185, 221-2
Turopolje, Noble Commune of, 193-6
Tuscany, last Grand Duke and Duchess of, 143
Two Sicilies, Queen of the, 143

Ugljan, Island of, 191
"Ugly Duchess" of Tyrol, the, 108
Uighurs, 201
Urbino, 45, 49, 55
Urgel, Bishop of, and Andorra, 58-63
Utrecht, Treaty of, 71, 109
Uz, John Peter, 122, 128

Vaduz, 75-6, 78
Valona, 152-3, 159, 188
Vatican City, State of the, 53, 65, 79-81
Velika Gorica, capital of Turopolje, 196
Venice, 47, 64, 160, 165, 167, 170-71, 185, 190-92, 213
Verdun, Treaty of, 103
Vienna, Congress of, 82, 110
Virbazar, 159-60
Vladikas (Prince-Bishops) of Montenegro, the, 161, 164-6, 266
Voltaire, 90-1, 96
Vorarlberg, 75

Wadi 'Atm, 224
Walloons, 106, 117
Wandrille, Abbey of S., 89
Wied, William of, Mbret of Albania, 152
Wilhelmina, Queen, 112, 114
Wight, Isle of, 71

Yahb-Allaha III, Nestorian Patriarch, 201-2, 206
Yemen, the, 227-8
"Yoldirim," Sultan (Bayazid I), 212, 217
York, Dukes of, 71-2
Yugoslavia, 153, 164, 188
Yvetot, Kingdom of, 87-100, 265-6

Zagreb, 193, 195
Zähringen, dynasty of, 128-9
Zante, 246-7
Zara, 153, 189-93
Zog, King, 151, 155, 157
Župan, the, of Turopolje, 195

270